Supervision:
Praxis and Purpose

Developing a critical model
of practice for those working with
children and young people
post Munro

**Brian Belton, Justin Hill, Tina Salter,
John Peaper**

Russell House Publishing

First published in 2011 by:
Russell House Publishing Ltd.
58 Broad Strteet
Lyme Regis
Dorset DT7 3QF

Tel: 01297-443948
Fax: 01297-442722
e-mail: help@russellhouse.co.uk

www.russellhouse.co.uk

© Brian Belton, Justin Hill, Tina Salter and John Peaper

The moral right of Brian Belton, Justin Hill, Tina Salter and John Peaper to be identified as the authors of this work has been asserted by them in accordance with The Copyright, Designs and Patents Act 1988.

British Library Cataloguing-in-publication Data:
A catalogue record for this book is available from the British Library.

ISBN: 978-1-905541-78-2

Typeset by TW Typesetting, Plymouth, Devon
Printed by IQ Laserpress, Aldershot

About Russell House Publishing

Russell House Publishing aims to publish innovative and valuable materials to help managers, practitioners, trainers, educators and students.

Our full catalogue covers: families, children and young people; drink, drugs and mental health; engagement and inclusion; workforce development in the human services; social work and youth work textbooks.

Full details can be found at www.russellhouse.co.uk and we are pleased to send out information to you by post. Our contact details are on this page.

We are always keen to receive feedback on publications and new ideas for future projects.

Contents

Preface

As the title suggests this book is for supervisors, and by association those using supervision (supervisees). The supervisor role is usually associated with the development and delivery of social work practice. However, supervision is widely practiced right across the 'people professions', which includes youth work, nursing and teaching. But there are supervisors operating in fields such as community work, and community development and learning, wherein the boundaries of youth work, teaching and social work are often blurred. Indeed, given the expectation of a duty of care, and child protection/safeguarding considerations, the context of supervision is far broader than any one profession. So while emphasis might differ, the demands of practice have huge areas of commonality.

As such, as far as is possible, the authors of this book have endeavoured to make the pages that follow useful across and, given the prevalence of interdisciplinary work, between professional contexts. This said, the writers come from a youth work background (although one of us is a qualified social worker), and although this means that many of their interests and concerns will share much with those involved in social work, we have necessarily approached the subject on the basis of our experience and expertise. However, as you will see, most of the theory that has informed supervision (including the supervision of youth workers and other professionals) has been developed within and out of social work, so although we have not set out to redress or suggest any imbalance, we hope that our efforts will add to, and perhaps prompt, a more eclectic pool of research.

Having gone to the trouble of justifying our contribution as youth workers to the analysis and development of supervision, it is the current reassessment of supervision practice within the major review of social work, the Munro Review, that has provided a significant prompt in terms of the development of this book. While focused on the English context Munro provides a global milestone as an example of analysis of exhaustive, comprehensive, consultative national research. It would be remiss of any future research over the international horizon to do any less than seriously consider the Review's findings and recommendations. As such, Munro will not only be a major consideration in terms of the shape of supervision practice within the UK, but will have an influence on supervisory approaches in youth and social work worldwide.

Background to the Munro Review

Dr Eileen Munro, a reader in social policy at the London School of Economics, writing in the *Independent on Sunday* (16 November 2008) argued that the reforms in social work organisation and practice, put in place following the abuse and murder of Victoria Climbié at the hands of her guardians in 2000, had been shown to be insufficient given the events that led up to the death of Peter Connelly ('Baby P') in Haringey in 2007. According to Munro the changes made had effectively failed to take into consideration that quality of front-line work is dependent on organisational quality and that underlying weaknesses in the same make front-line error more probable. She argued that a chance combination of these faults can lay the ground for strategic and practice calamities.

For Munro, the audit and inspection systems did not enhance the transparency of practice, as they placed emphasis on the simply measured standards, like meetings held or forms filled in, almost regardless if these provided sturdily reasoned decisions based on reliable information and clearly articulated, logical decision-making. Munro went on to state that psychological research demonstrates that people are not good at subjugating personal bias, and that social workers need regular critical supervision to guarantee their partiality might not distort assessments. To exemplify this situation she cited the mistake of the social worker in the Baby P case seeing the mother as compliant in the face of evidence to the contrary (Baby P's continuous injury that occurred only while he was in his mother's care). Munro asserted that robust supervision should have questioned this erroneous appraisal.

According to Munro, social work managers cutting back on casework supervision might be seen in the same light as hospital managers deciding to save costs on operating theatre sterilisation. As the latter is likely to result in a higher incidence of patient infection, so the former will result in a rise in poor/a lack of appropriate reasoning.

Good practice, Munro argued, requires assessment being understood as an ongoing process which continually reviews and revises how cases are seen and responded to. For her the question of how to make better judgements and decisions is vital.

Following the commission by the Secretary of State for Education, the Right Honourable Michael Gove MP, in the *The Munro Review of Child Protection (Part One)* Munro (now Professor) advised that the Social Work Reform Board:

> . . . *produce standards for employers of social workers, to include commitment to a culture of regular professional supervision and continuing professional development as the best ways of supporting social workers and improving practice.*
>
> 2010: 8

Later (ibid.: 17, 1.28) she explains that reflective supervision involves the supervisor helping the supervisee '. . . *notice what is happening and revise their reasoning*' and that supervision demands that those involved retain '. . . *an open and questioning mindset*' and that this '*requires regular, challenging supervision*' (ibid.: 18, 1.29).

The Munro Review of Child Protection (Part One) the subsequent *Interim* and *Final* reports provide a comprehensive review and systems analysis of child protection procedures and management. Within this, supervision is taken to be a crucial element in the development of good practice. But as can be understood from the above, supervision practice has been stymied by bureaucratic exigencies and poor understanding of psychological considerations latent in practice conditions and situation; while supervision might have reflective content, without professional judgement (reason premised on evidence) this becomes little more than a speculative exercise. However, the use of evidence needs mediation. As Munro (2011: 54, 4.16) highlights, if workers:

> . . . *simply use evidence to shore up their initial assumptions, rather than to understand the range and complexity of relevant factors, such a resource may exacerbate poor practice.*

Theory is often taken on in much the same way; identified and shoe horned into practice in the anticipation that this will show practice to be informed by theory. Unfortunately this means that by and large theory shapes practice as workers do little more than demonstrate paucity in terms of professional judgement.

The focus of Munro was the strengthening of the social work profession, to put practitioners into a better position to make well-informed judgements based on up-to-date evidence in the best interests of children and free from unnecessary bureaucracy and regulation. This builds on the work of Lord Laming's Progress Report (March 2009) and the Social Work Task Force, drawing on the evidence submitted to the reviews.

Munro's recommendations are aimed at creating long-term change, arguing for a fundamental shift in the way the system works, to enable professionals to focus on the needs of children, young people and families. The Government committed to work closely with a group of professionals from across the children's sector to develop a full response to Munro's recommendations which, in short, mark *'a move from compliance to a learning culture'* which will require practitioners *'to be given more scope to exercise professional judgment'* together with *'a more determined and robust management at the front line to support the development of professional confidence'* (see http://www.education.gov.uk/munroreview/). The latter includes the development of *evidence based* supervision practice.

What the supervisor will gain from this book

In the light of Munro's review this book seeks to provide a direction for supervision practice founded on the reasoned review of practice, which is inherent in the development of professional judgment and the quality assurance of front-line practice. This has produced the most thorough theoretical review of the theory of supervision practice yet published; this statement is probably about as clear an indication as possible that the work does not aim to provide the reader with a 'how to' text. Although a great deal can be picked up about the traditions and methods deployed in supervision, what follows seeks to begin to address a clear gap in the practice and understanding of supervision, particularly in the youth work context, although the pages that follow are also pertinent to supervisory practice in other fields, such as social work. For many years youth work has been informed by social work theory and practice, it is hoped that this book will play a role in returning that compliment.

While the book does not a provide a primer in supervision, neither does it ask for a massive knowledge of supervision, as the bedrock of theory of the latter is explained, reviewed and analysed. At the same time the work includes a great deal in terms of description of the character of the delivery of supervision, its purpose and effectiveness. No one taking the time to read the book will walk away from it mystified about what supervision might be, does or is capable of doing. Indeed, if you consider the approaches and the ideas presented with an open mind all the contributors are confident you will have a head start to becoming an able or a more effective supervisor, less prone to the pitfalls that are probably inherent in the discipline. But you can also learn from the ideas and arguments we as writers and practitioners offer; it would also be negligent of us not to invite you into the debate; as such you might find some of what follows more or less provocative. However, that is how learning is incited, via the ignition of an inclination to argue for better practice. That might be thought of as our (readers and authors) collective reward.

This said, for those relatively new to supervision it might be helpful to read Chapters 3 and 4 after other content. For those unfamiliar with youth work practice it might be useful to read Appendix 1.

Structure, direction and theoretical underpinning

Each chapter has been written in order that they might be read as freestanding statements or as a continuous narrative relating to practice. Hence the reader can start at the beginning and read this book to a logical end point or it can be dipped into according to need or mood. Whatever your choice, the ideas and theory encompassed are best not left to one reading. It is envisaged that the book will be a constant source of referral and development for those interested in questioning and so developing their practice, whether as supervisor or supervisee, in youth or social work, counselling or any professional setting.

As Munro suggests, the basic model of supervision has not been subjected to anything like sustained/energetic critical examination. Its assumptions and claims have been almost unproblematically accepted and deployed in the professional context. This of course obviously demonstrates paucity in terms of professional judgement and as such raises concerns with regard to discerning practice.

Many of these ideas, which together both describe and inform practice, are sometimes taken as the 'theoretical basis' of supervision, creak in the modern context as their therapeutic or dated management underpinnings become exposed in the practical demands of the contemporary professional environment. They have been stretched and manipulated until, at this point in time, in many situations and contexts, as Munro testifies, they are unfit for purpose.

The response of supervision delivery in a time of recession, resource scarcity or 'austerity' to understandable demands for 'value for money' and meaningful outcomes have not produced the necessary development in the paradigm. While other approaches have emerged, for example mentoring and coaching, varying levels of disorientation in terms of purpose have been evident to the extent that in some instances it is hard for the neutral observer to say what exactly is going on in any particular coaching, mentoring or supervision encounter. Vague, woolly and subjective explanations or interpretations, often premised on a range of self contradictory assumptions and opinions, all seem to gravitate towards a direct bureaucratic or therapeutic root, etched in the assumption that what is 'wrong' can be 'treated' by way of ticking boxes, a talking cure or some fuzzy jumble of the same. Such supposition has no secure basis in fact, in that it has never been substantiated by rigorous research or analysis. For all this, the remedial model becomes confused with or pre-eminent over the need to 'get the job done'; the trajectory of the supervision appears to be dominated by the aim to make the supervisee 'feel better' or 'happier' via, what is in effect, a rather sterile form of Platonic questioning or merely show that targets (the point of which has sometimes evaporated or been misunderstood) have been met. While perhaps a pay rise (maybe equal to the cost of the supply of supervision?) or more time off might cause people to feel even more happy and lead to them feeling better still, the fact that supervision is put in place to aid effective and efficient delivery of services is frequently lost.

Supervision seems to mean different things to different people and it might be argued that this diversity of opinions and approaches has its strengths. But how can we 'do' supervision without being quite sure of what it is or that all of us, when talking about supervision, mean the same thing? It is part of the aim of this book to address this situation: to mark something of a boundary (not an impermeable barrier) around practice. For instance, while there might be points at which practitioners are in need of referral to therapy and the supervisor might even recommend the same, this book will argue that supervision can't be therapy and remain supervision. This type of 'role confusion' needs to be avoided. In a similar vein Munro (2011a: 115, 7.33) states:

> *A common experience amongst social workers is that the few supervision opportunities are dominated by a managerial need to focus on performance, for example, throughput, case closure, adhering to timescales and completion of written records. This leaves little time for thoughtful consideration of what is happening in the lives of children and their families.*

Just as supervision may be experienced as therapeutic by a supervisee but is not in fact therapy, supervision might arguably be viewed as part of the function of management, while not becoming a management exercise of itself. As such supervision, by way of both supervisor and supervisee vigilance, needs to build in checks and balances that literally keep the process on line.

The Supervision Boundary

Management	Supervision	Therapy

This book invites the reader to make a start on disentangling these issues, via a questioning of the taken-for-granted notions that have grown into a sort of credo from their seeding during the 1960s. At the same time, calling on the experience and practice of professionals, the pages that follow work towards the generation of a clear and developmental orientation for future practice. This links purpose and function to current social expectations, thus providing a realistic and vibrant resource for effective and efficient practice, in a time wherein conditions demand nothing less.

References

Laming, Lord (2009) *The Protection of Children in England: A Progress Report*. HMSO.

Munro, E. (2008) Lessons Learnt, Boxes Ticked, Families Ignored. *Independent on Sunday*, 16 November.

Munro, E. (2010) *The Munro Review of Child Protection Part One: A Systems Analysis*. DoE.

Munro, E. (2011) *The Munro Review of Child Protection Interim Report: The Child's Journey*. DoE.

Munro, E. (2011a) *The Munro Review of Child Protection: Final Report. A child-centred System*. DoE.

About the Authors

The contributors to this book come from a wide range of backgrounds and interests in supervision and youth work. This being the case, together they provide a diverse but consistently critical analysis of the theory, function and delivery of supervision.

Brian Belton

Coming from an East London/English Gypsy background, Brian entered youth work partly as an escape from the hooligan/gang life of the late 1960s/early 1970s docklands. While working in youth work related situations around the world, including Israel, the Falkland Islands, the USA, Thailand, Hong Kong, Zambia, South Africa, China and Canada, Brian's interest in identity and ethnicity flourished and today he is an internationally recognised authority on Gypsy Ethnicity and youth work having written widely on those subjects, delivering papers most recently in the USA, Greece, Sweden and Slovenia as well as around the UK. Brian has been developing a growing network of practitioners and academics concerned with the exploration of youth work and Islam. Brian gained a BSc at City University, an MA at the University of Essex and was awarded his doctorate by the University of Kent. He is now a Senior Lecturer with responsibility for supervision at the YMCA George Williams College in London, a leading qualifying agency for professional youth work. Brian is currently coordinating the professionalism of youth work with the Commonwealth Youth Project, in six South East Asian Nations, including Malaysia, Bangladesh and Sri Lanka.

Other publications include: *Bubbles, Hammers and Dreams* (1997) Breedon; *Questioning Gypsy Identity: Ethnic Narratives in Britain and America* (2005) AltaMira Press; *Gypsy and Traveller Ethnicity: The social generation of an Ethnicity* (2005) Routledge; *Black Routes : Legacy of African Diaspora* (2007) Hansib; *The Ryder Lions* (2007) Pennant; *Developing Critical Youth Work Theory* (2009) Sense; *Radical Youth Work: Developing Critical Perspectives and Professional Judgement* (2009) Russell House; *All Change!: Romani Studies Through Romani Eyes* (2010) University of Hertfordshire Press (with Damian Le Bas, Thomas Acton); *Differentiated Teaching and Learning in Youth Work* (2010) *Sense* (with Simon Frost).

Justin Hill

Justin Hill is Chief Executive of St Helens YMCA. He has worked at a governance level with services for young people, including sitting on the children's trust boards in Lincolnshire and Merseyside. He has run a foyer project in London, was a housing manager for a 16+ hostel, was deputy chief executive of Lincolnshire YMCA, and was a member of the Social Inclusion Programme Group of the European Alliance of YMCAs. He has recently finished his EdD at Nottingham University, where he has been studying the educational philosophy of Martin Buber and the practice of work supervision in English YMCAs.

John Peaper

John Peaper was born in East London in 1966 and grew up in Newham. As a field worker, John has turned his hand to a wealth of Youth and Community work related projects. This has ranged from generic and detached work to specialist project work, which has included working with young offenders, children/adults with autism, outdoor education and sports coaching.

With over 20 years of youth work experience John now teaches at the YMCA George Williams College where he graduated with BA (Hons) Degree in 1995.

Beyond his teaching commitments, John is still actively involved in a range of voluntary community based projects and has a vast network of youth work contacts throughout East London and Essex where much of this work takes place.

Over the past ten years, John gained valuable experience working as a professional Supervisor and currently delivers training relating this within and beyond the College.

Tina Salter

Tina graduated from the Oasis Youth Ministry Course in 1993 and has since completed a Diploma in Mentoring at Leeds Metropolitan University and a Masters Degree in Coaching and Mentoring Practice at Oxford Brookes University.

Tina has worked in the field of informal education for more than 21 years in both the voluntary and statutory sectors. Latterly she was team leader for an inclusion project based in Southwark where she specialised in mentoring and small group work with young people at risk of exclusion and offending.

Tina is one of the Programme Organisers for the BA (Hons) Distance Learning Programme at the YMCA George Williams College, with specific responsibility for student matters. She also teaches on both the distance learning and full-time modes of study at the College. An article based on her MA research was published in the *International Journal of Evidence Based Coaching and Mentoring*, Special Issue No.2, November 2008 entitled, 'Exploring current thinking within the field of coaching on the role of supervision'.

Introduction

Supervision is a notion that can be understood in a number of ways according to purpose and context. Supervision might be taken as part of general management, an interaction that is part of line management. Casework supervision by line managers is something recognised in social work as is discussing casework and/or project work with someone outside one's organisation. However, people are supervised when working towards the achievement of corporate objectives in various situations and supervisors might be understood as dealing with employee welfare and employment issues. Supervision is linked to regularly scheduled meetings, forms of crisis intervention, dialogue in structured settings, en passant dialogue, etc. However, what follows refers to:

- The supervision of professional practitioners.
- For the betterment of practice.
- Broadly within welfare and care related professions.
- More explicitly social and youth work milieu.

In what follows, debating the merits and differences between non-managerial (out-of-organisation) and managerial (internal) supervision has been largely avoided as the overall analysis is concerned specifically with supervision as a means of developing professional judgement by way of the reasoned review of practice, which can, and probably should, be facilitated in both managerial and non-managerial contexts. This might simplistically be thought of as a reflective case-work supervision, however as the reader will discover, the direction of analysis will provide more possibilities than traditional orientations of this kind.

Learning from other professions

The common ground between youth work and social work is the overriding concern for the welfare of the client. Working with young people, just like social workers, youth workers need to be aware of and responsive to the legislation and policy relating to child protection and safeguarding: youth workers are also subject to the expectation of a duty of care and are often involved with young people considered to be 'at risk' or vulnerable. Alongside social workers, youth workers can now be found employed across the child care sector, in schools and further education settings. While youth workers are often associated with leisure activities, and can be found in play work and leisure provision, in terms of child related issues, roles and concerns there is a substantial overlap between youth and social worker functions. Although youth workers, according to situation and role, do not always have the clear duties and expectations in law that social workers have and are, in the main focused on preventative strategies rather than crisis intervention.

At the same time, youth work, being the younger and smaller of the two professions, has not generated the theoretical and practice muscle of social work. As such, it has traditionally drawn on social work practice theory to inform delivery, codes of conduct and ethics. However, because youth work also has a relationship with social, informal and political education, its traditions and function have also been informed by theories of education, learning and teaching. This said, social workers involved with young people have also embraced informal and social educational approaches within their helping and welfare functions. For an overview of the character of youth work see Appendix 1.

This being the case, as ideas and practice have been borrowed, adapted and translated from social work to youth work, so the growing body of literature emanating from youth work can be usefully modified and interpreted into social work. Most practitioners will be open to this. Indeed many would be familiar with crossing such disciplinary boundaries. Youth work and social work are informed by classic writing on childhood education/experience and counselling, emphasising the place of empathy and person centred approaches (Friedrich Froebel, Carl Rogers). Nursing practice in relation to compassion and detachment have much to tell both professions, while what has become known as 'police trauma' has resonance for those who have spent great parts of their career dealing with particularly violent and aggressive young people. It is clear that in the field of 'people work', we might miss a great many potential intellectual and practically useful resources by maintaining a sort of 'monotheistic' approach to theory and practice experience.

However, the vast majority of the literature and theory relating to supervision has emanated from social work practice. Youth work has largely adopted this material as the basis of its delivery of supervision. At the same time, in terms of young people, both youth and social work share a primary focus on welfare and safeguarding. That said, youth workers do not have the same legal status as social workers and have traditionally been more concerned with young people's (formal, informal and the margin in between) pursuit of leisure, recreational and socially educative activities than their counterparts in social work. This does not imply that social workers are not involved in similar endeavours, they clearly are (as are, amongst others, teachers, play and community workers, librarians, sports coaches, workers across the leisure industry, members of the clergy, specialist nurses and an appreciable number of police and prison officers working with young offenders). But youth workers have traditionally been specialist arbiters in the social education and interactive recreation, occupied in and devoted to these areas of youth experience.

Over the last few years a body of theory made specific to youth work has been emerging (for example Buchroth and Parkin, 2010). However, the literature surrounding youth work has traditionally been largely narrative, anecdotal (Williamson, 1991) instructional (for instance Sapin, 2008; Fitzsimons, Hope and Russell, 2011) and, at times, almost apocryphal (Wilson, 1985). There have been stoic attempts to forge an ancestry of youth work from historic patchworks of accounts, records, chronologies and approaches of diverse youth movements. The moral, missionary, political and humanitarian niches and enclaves, which have made the attention, redemption, reformation, education, indoctrination and permutations of all of these, for the young their target (Davies, 1999; Gilchrist, Jeffs, Spence and Walker, 2009; Gilchrist, Jeffs, Spence, Stanton and Walker, 2011). Other work has provided a sort of fusion of much of the above, and the best of this has translated into the social work realm (Jeffs and Smith, 1987, 1999). Something more than manuals, this literature presents a kind of usefully directive philosophy, which until relatively recently has been mainstay of thinking, supporting youth work practice and providing a rational for its direction and development.

However, because of the relative paucity of youth work theory, practice has to some extent become dependent on theory drawn from social work training and counselling. This has been augmented with a range of group work approaches, elements of learning theory, fundamental behavioural psychology, basic sociology, policy analysis and some rudimentary law. This situation, together with the very generic nature of youth work practice, has served, occasionally, to blur the divide between the two professions. Indeed, teachers, parents and others involved in the lives of young people often find it impossible to distinguish between the roles played by youth workers and social workers in relation to young people.

Vague labels like 'informal' education or 'community' development applied sporadically to youth work has done more to confuse than clarify this state of affairs. Maybe this is because youth workers (like many teachers) in reality vacillate between formal and informal methods (although what is formal to one person might be informal to another). However, it is probably incorrect to argue that young people have traditionally approached youth workers looking to be educated by them. The personification of education of young people, in our society, is the teacher. In the better part of four decades involved in youth work all over Britain, never has a parent approached me and asked how their child's education is going. Of all the thousands of youth workers I have known, not one has told me of such an experience.[1] With the exception of youth work managers, administrators, academics and a few well rehearsed politicians, the most common enquiries about the young people I have worked with have been related in part to their behaviour and enjoyment, but overwhelmingly to their welfare.

This aside, unlike teachers, youth workers have no duty to educate although they are locked into legal expectations of a duty of care. Furthermore, young people have not, in the main, in the last half century or so in any number, voluntarily got involved in youth work with the aim of indulging in education. By far and away, the most positive experiences of youth work related by young people, the memories of adults and the

---

[1] Apart from some working in school settings – who are often mistakenly taken to be teachers.

informal accounts of practitioners are described as 'fun'.[2] As such, while incarnations of youth work might be 'safe' and 'educational', the mass affirmation of youth work is its capacity to provide enjoyment, excitement and fulfilment via a caring attitude and approach.

It is expressly not part of the purpose of this book to argue that youth work and social work are twin occupations. The case work approach, legal positioning and the catalyst for social work intervention being based on prescribed thresholds alone, apart from other considerations, create a clear divide. But, in relation to young people, because of the shared social expectations of youth and social work, the similarity of their primary focus, policy and legal concerns, theoretical grounding and their presumed societal functions that these occupations are presumed to and actually do fulfil, they are closely related professions in terms of general best practice ambitions and outcomes. This is why the pages which follow are pertinent to both professional groups.

Praxis

The spine of this book, although it will hardly be mentioned after this introduction, is supervision 'praxis'; the functional application or exercise of this practice. At first glance that looks a bit too straightforward for a book of this size, but it is not 'Ten Steps on How to be a Supervisor' nor a rough guide to the same. What is provided is a critical analysis of and a theoretical underpinning to what Munro (2011) sees supervision as providing; a *space for critical reflection*. For her this is *'essential for reducing the risk of errors in professionals' reasoning'*. However in the same section (15) she makes the point that, *'There is a growing body of relevant research to support professionals' reasoning'* and there is a *'need to make best use of evidence'* (ibid.: 11–12). This indicates that these considerations need to be implicated within the supervision process. However, a more definite case for the use of evidence in supervision was made by Munro, (2011a: 8, 13):

> ... *a local authority wishing to implement a particular evidence-based way of working with children and families needs to consider what changes might be needed in the training, supervision, IT support and monitoring to enable this to be carried out effectively.*

As such, the analysis throughout this book has been premised on the same; that supervision should be actively informed by theory and be based on evidence drawn from practice. As such, what is proposed is a move away from reflection that run the risk of moving into the realm of conjecture and so driving practice on the basis of supposition, assumption and, in worse case scenarios, fantasy.

For Munro, supervision involves working with practitioners to draw out the reasoning

---

[2]This differs in some parts of Europe, Asia, Africa and America where youth work encompasses a deal of vocational and not unusually extra-curricular formal education. However, in much of the USA (and other national contexts) youth work is practically synonymous with areas of social work, apart from status and legal considerations. From a global perspective youth work is no one thing, but it is, overall, intrinsically bound to welfare considerations that in many non-industrial areas is largely expressed from a rights perspective.

behind their judgements for review (37, 3.14) and argues (calling on Gilovich, Griffin, and Kahneman, 2008) that:

> ... *intuitive judgments are vulnerable to predictable types of error and critical challenge by others is needed to help social workers catch such biases and correct them.*
>
> 38, 3.15

This might be thought of as part of the process that creates professional judgement. As Munro puts it, the need to *'be challenged by others is reinforced by the fact that intuitive reasoning "generates feelings of certitude"'* (38–9, 3.18).

In effect this means that there is a limit to what personal reflection can achieve. Reflection is understood as a necessary aspect of supervision. But reflection without consideration ('beholding', 'keeping in mind', 'taking account of') via an actively critical and challenging review of action, implicating practice evidence, is likely to be largely speculation.

To really get a grasp of what something, say supervision, is and how it is done, you need to do more than produce a description of supervision premised on statements about what it is. All that would do is tell you what someone or a group of people thought or said about what supervision is and its purpose. Much of the literature appertaining to the subject is a bit like this. However, to gain a solid focus on the praxis of supervision you will need to look at its theoretical basis; what its proponents claim it is able to achieve and then expose this to logical questioning and analysis. In effect this is a process of enquiry rather than mere explanation (although the procedure will certainly serve to be explanatory) by way of the deconstruction of the current paradigm.

If this exercise is effective, it will not only expose what supervision (or any set of ideas or practices) is and does, but will throw up its flaws. This will enable supervisors to develop or improve existing practice and, if supervision is like any other collection of notions, assumptions, beliefs, customs, skills and techniques, and there is no reason to believe it is not, eventually move forward the evolution of or replace the existing 'church' of supervision with a new and more effective, relevant paradigm. This is serving supervision in much the same way as supervision might most effectively serve practice in that it is challenging *feelings of certitude* that Munro argues are alluring to those who might be operating in situations involving uncertainty. For her, raw intuition (what one is left with without rigorous examination) can lead to confidence about judgments which cause practitioners to be resistant to questioning or the suggestion of a change of attitude or tack. This being the case, according to Munro (2011) with regard to supervision *critical appraisal* needs to be understood as fundamental to *good practice in reducing error* (39, 3.18). Citing Turnell, (in press) she argues that those involved in child protection:

> ... *are constantly making judgments that impinge on the rights of parents to be with and relate to their children and the parallel right of children to their parents. The stakes are high and child protection decision making needs to be as explicit as possible and be available for review and scrutiny.*

This sets the mood for this book; scrutiny and review is expected of supervision and as such supervision needs to be exposed to the same sort of treatment/respect.

Investigating supervision

As Munro points out, the Social Work Task Force and the Social Work Reform Board have understood that supervision is part of what makes good practice possible (2011: 34, 3.2). However, the purpose of supervision is to provide a situation and means to reflect on practice (see Schon, 1983). Overall, supervision is seen as a tool which, via the reflective process, will enhance the delivery and quality of practice and as a corollary augment job satisfaction and feelings of personal efficacy. But, the crucial although underlying assumption in this model is that reflection provides a sort of 'royal road' to look at and understand actual events in order to come up with better and/or more appropriate ways of working with and relating to other professionals and clients. However reflection, relying as it does on the approximations of personal and relative perception, mediated by the fragile and fickle character of memory, being prone to personal life-scripts, imagination, and bias, can hardly be touted as a sturdy means of relaying the reality of actual events and often complex social situations.

Added to this, Munro (2011: 40) draws attention to the Social Work Reform Board Capabilities Framework and it sees social workers as requiring ability to:

> . . . *demonstrate professional commitment by taking responsibility for their conduct, practice and learning, with support through supervision.*

The question that is begged from this statement is what the nature and content of supervision might be. This seems to be answered by the subsequent contention that social workers are also understood to have the capacity to:

> . . . *apply the principles of critical thinking and reasoned discernment. They identify, distinguish, evaluate and integrate multiple sources of knowledge and evidence. These include practice evidence, their own practice experience, service user and carer experience together with research-based, organisational, policy and legal knowledge. They use critical thinking augmented by creativity and curiosity.*
>
> Munro, 2011, 41

The emphasis on supervision having this multifaceted quality is confirmed with regard to the expectations about professional leadership, wherein it is anticipated that responsibility for '. . . *professional learning and development of others*' (ibid.) will be facilitated through supervision that includes *assessment of practice* (Munro, 2011: 41).

For Munro (2011: 48, 3.45)

> *A working life given over to distracted involvement does not allow for the integration of experience.*

As such practice experience alone is not enough:

It needs to be allied to reflection – time and attention given to mulling over the experience and learning from it. This is often best achieved in conversation with others, in supervision . . . or in discussions with colleagues. (ibid)

Referencing Klein (2000) Munro identifies four key ways in which experts learn:

1. Engaging in deliberate practice, and setting specific goals and evaluation criteria.
2. Compiling extensive experience banks.
3. Obtaining feedback that is accurate, diagnostic, and reasonably timely.
4. Enriching their experience by reviewing prior experiences to derive new insights and lessons from mistakes.

So, while supervision includes reflecting on experience, to be effective it needs to be more than this. As such, the supervisor needs to be more than a 'sounding board' or a question asking machine. This being the case, the supervisor role needs to be catalytic and critical more than passive and impartial as is perhaps sometimes concluded, as they, the supervisor, has a responsibility within the nexus of service delivery. A perhaps largely ignored issue connected with the need for clarity of purpose in supervision practice is the possible position of the supervisor in law. Jenkins (2007a, 2007b) demonstrates that the supervisor, depending on employment/contract arrangements, is potentially accountable to anyone who has a legitimate interest or concern in the supervisor's practice via duty of care. However, regardless of employment status, the supervisor will nearly always have an ethical duty towards the supervisee's clients.

For all this, supervision also needs to be more than a reflective process because the accuracy of personalised raw reflection is (as we have seen) doubtful. How can we build effective/efficient practice unless we can begin with a reliable perspective of what we are doing or what we have done previously? It is this endeavour which has motivated the writing of this book.

What follows was written by academic and professional colleagues who, in combination, orientate the reader in terms of what supervision is, its uses, aims, claims and basis. At the same time, taken as a whole, the writers look to give something of an impetus in terms of developing a more cogent and appropriate direction for supervision practice, providing the elements for a more professional foundation for the creation of what might be recognised as a definite discipline.

According to Munro (2011: 53, 4.11):

The two major functions of supervision are the management oversight of caseloads and the professional casework supervision of practice . . . managerial oversight often predominates and that too little attention is given to professional supervision.

At the same time much supervision is *'overly concerned with management issues'* rather than *'professional casework analysis'*. (ibid.: 94, 6.3). Citing Howe (1992) Munro argues that understanding of this asymmetry has been around for some time in the shape of tension between *notions of professional expertise* and:

> . . . *managerial concerns of a hierarchical bureaucracy attempting to respond to a heavy bombardment rate, fearful of child abuse scandals on their doorstep.*

For Howe a *growing concern* existed that this tension was:

> . . . *being resolved inappropriately by tighter managerial control over practitioners, with more emphasis on procedures for child protection but with less support for enhancing professional tasks.*
>
> Ibid.: 53, 4.11

Supervision practice needs to be premised much more on the honing of professional judgement, which obliges a move away from the resort to largely bureaucratic or administration led techniques. But at the other extreme there needs to be a more definite rigour applied to supervision practice that avoids the nebulous, pseudo-psychoanalytical models often deployed in the context of youth work. The latter have, since the 1960s, merged with an American West Coast ethos, that has splurged out New Age adages, couched in vaguely religious terms, spiced in a sort ersatz Eastern verbiage, which has produced, at times, a sort of shallow halo of mysticism around the subject, conjured more out of legend (see for example Christian and Kitto, 1987: 1.) claim and conjecture, than solid rational argument or the critical examination of practice.

This being the case, what follows constitutes a critical analysis of what is said to happen, while asking what fails to happen (that should perhaps happen) in supervision. But it also examines how things occur and the way that ideas are applied. Together, this is the 'praxis' of supervision; the way the process applies knowledge and the manner in which supervision is carried out with this knowledge as background. Further, the book asks questions of this applied knowledge, both in terms of its relevance and overall fitness for purpose relative to what might be realistically expected of supervision.

In Chapter 1 John Peaper and Justin Hill look at the theoretical basis of supervision and from this identify its purposes and aims. This is the most in-depth analysis of the foundations of supervision and reflective practice published to date, providing a comprehensive overview of the evolution and delivery of the discipline.

Tina Salter then looks at the potential and actual role of supervision in supporting coaching practice. This chapter aims to show the relevance of supervision to the rapidly developing field of coaching, and in the process reinforces the case for a new paradigm of supervision in other areas, including youth work and social work. It has been written in contexts of initial resistance by coaches to being supervised, and of coaches becoming increasingly involved in both youth work and social work, for example in delivering life skills coaching in gaps left by the retreat service provision due to cuts in funding. Tina examines the connection that supervision has with similar incarnations of reflective practice. It will offer a perspective on the character and the range techniques and responses that might be placed under the banner of reflective practice. At the same time this will involve an analysis of contemporary approaches to the supervision of coaches, and ways in which practitioners and agencies perceive this developing.

Overall, this asks questions about supervision's significance relative to coaching, proffering a view of supervision and coaching via their latent and actual relationship. The basic connections of supervision, coaching, and psychotherapy will also be considered. This will facilitate an analysis of the potential for supervision practice withing coaching.

The chapter provides a picture of the character and practical application of supervision while presenting some of the concerns about its validity and function.

Chapter 3 highlights the importance of dialogue as the fabric of supervision, demonstrating how the interaction of supervision can illicit educational purpose and direction. Dialogue has long been seen as the central tool in youth work and as such has been a major focus of supervision practice in this arena. Justin Hill and Brian Belton will develop a more in-depth understanding of the character of dialogical interaction but take this on to argue that dialectical relations can take learning associations, within the supervision setting, onto a more definite plain of insightful understanding and educational endeavour. This enables not only the facilitation of considered practice but creates new directions out of mutually questioning encounters.

Chapter 4 by Hill and Belton looks at the educational purposes and functions of supervision in the light of Martin Buber's philosophy of dialogue. Buber provides a definite platform on which to develop a review of current theory. This offers a firm and alternative path for the delivery of supervision, one which propounds a clearer, more philosophically but also practically grounded, explanation of the connection between supervisor and supervisee and the task and role of the supervisor as an educator, but who is ready to learn about the supervisor's practice from the supervisee.

Four concepts central to Buber's educational philosophy are identified that are also of significant potential interest and relevance to the practice of work supervision.

The four themes concern: the encouragement and promotion of dialogue – both within and beyond the educative relationship; authority in educational encounters; Buber's concept of responsibility; and the example of the educator. In addition to being material concepts within Buber's philosophy, each of these themes is contestable – in that there is a plausible alternative perspective in each case.

The themes identified are not discrete but are interrelated within Buber's philosophy. It is, however, possible to distinguish each theme clearly without distorting Buber's message. The following four sections explain each theme in detail, elucidating both the Buberian and the alternative perspective.

In the final two chapters Brian Belton examines the nature of the fundamental building blocks of supervision. Firstly, an analysis of eye-witnessing, Brian will demonstrate that human memory, as a function of mind and a product of perception, is fragile and unreliable. As such, it becomes obvious that reflection is characteristically a process of distortion in terms of rebuilding a picture of past events. This being the case the question is begged as to how reflective practice above can provide a reliable basis on which to advance understanding of professional intervention.

Chapter 6 looks to develop a practical but critical overview of practice. Out of this a more difinitive direction for practice is evolved.

References

Buchroth, I. and Parkin, C. (Eds.) (2010) *Using Theory in Youth and Community Work Practice (Empowering Youth and Community Work Practice).* Learning Matters.

Christian, C. and Kitto, J. (1987) *The Theory and Practice of Supervision.* YMCA George Williams College.

Davies, B. (1999) *From Voluntaryism to Welfare State (History of the Youth Service in England).* National Youth Agency.

Davies, B. (1999) *From Thatcherism to New Labour (History of the Youth Service in England) Volume 2. 1979–1999,* National Youth Agency.

Fitzsimons, A., Hope, M. and Russell, J. (2011) *Empowerment and Participation in Youth Work (Empowering Youth and Community Work Practice).* Learning Matters.

Gilchrist, R., Hodgson, T., Jeffs, T., Spence, J., Stanton, N. and Walker, J. (2011) *Reflecting on the Past: Essays in the History of Youth and Community Work.* Russell House Publishing.

Gilchrist, R., Jeffs, T., Spence, J. and Walker, J. (2009) *Essays in the History of Youth and Community Work: Discovering The Past.* Russell House Publishing.

Gilovich, T., Griffin D. and Kahneman, D. (Eds.) (2008) *Heuristics and Biases: The Psychology of Intuitive Judgment.* Cambridge University Press.

Howe, D. (1992) Child Abuse and The Bureaucratisation of Social Work. *The Sociological Review*, 40, 491.

Jeffs, T. and Smith, M.K. (Eds.) (1987) *Youth Work (Practical Social Work Series).* Palgrave Macmillan.

Jeffs, T. and Smith, M.K. (Eds.) (1999) *Informal Education.* Education Now Publishing Co-operative.

Jenkins, P. (2007) *Counselling, Psychotherapy and the Law.* 2nd edn, Sage.

Jenkins, P. (2007) Supervisors in the Dock? Supervision and the Law. In Tudor, K. and Worrall, M. (Eds.) *Freedom to Practise.* Volume 2. PCCS.

Klein, G. (2000) *Sources of Power: How People Make Decisions.* MIT Press.

Munro, E. (2011) *The Munro Review of Child Protection Interim Report: The Child's Journey.* DoE.

Munro, E. (2011a) *The Munro Review of Child Protection: Final Report. A Child-centred System.* DoE.

Nathan, A. and Nathan, J. (1996) The Supervision of Child Protection Work. *British Journal of Social Work*, 26, 357–7.

Sapin, K. (2008) *Essential Skills for Youth Work Practice.* Sage Publications.

Schon, D.A. (1983) *The Reflective Practitioner: How Professionals Think in Action.* Basic Books.

Social Work Task Force (2009) *Building a Safe and Confident Future* (available online at: http://www.education.gov.uk/publications/eOrderingDownload/01114_2009DOM_EN.pdf)

Turnell, A. (in press) *Building Safety in Child Protection Practice: Working with a Strengths and Solution Focus in an Evironment of Risk.* Palgrave.

Williamson, H. (1991) *The Lifechance Project: Social Action Work With Disadvantaged Young People.* University of Wales College of Cardiff, Social Research Unit.

Wilson, P. (1985) *Gutter Feelings.* HarperCollins.

Supervision: An Overview of Theory, Use, Impact and Purpose

Justin Hill and John Peaper

Munro (2011: 53, 4.11) points out the significance the Social Work Task Force placed on supervision, understanding it as:

> *. . . an integral element of social work practice not an add-on. Through it social workers review their day-to-day practice and decision making, plan their learning and development as professionals, and work through the considerable emotional and personal demands the job often places on them.*

It is hard to argue with this. However, in order to deliver appropriate supervision one must have a working notion of what it is and what it is meant to achieve. For Munro supervision is, 'a core mechanism for helping social workers to critically reflect on the understanding they are forming in the practice situation' (ibid.: 53, 4.10). At the same time it is a time and space for:

> *. . . considering their emotional response and whether this is adversely affecting their reasoning, and for making decisions about how best to help.*

Here there are two concomitant considerations that involve developing situational insight (knowledge, understanding) and awareness of attitude (personal reaction/ response). As such, it is clear that supervision needs to strike a balance between exploration of the personal/psychological and the dynamics of front-line practice. However, supervision content has other facets. According to Munro:

> *Supervision offers reflective time and the practice framework encourages this through a critical and theoretical engagement . . .*
>
> Ibid.: 109

Supervision, from this perspective, needs to be critical. It is hardly possible to develop a critique without a level of interrogative activity. As such, it is clear that effective supervision of this type demands that both supervisor and supervisee are active participants, ready to examine, analyse and question. But, as can be seen, supervision also needs theoretical content, which will equally be subjected to critical analysis. It is with this in mind that this chapter will examine the theory surrounding and informing supervision practice via an analysis of the subject's research horizon.

Supervision is delivered and understood in a number of contexts, and although for the sake of brevity and focus, this book concentrates on practice within the youth work arena, research into the subject has mainly arisen from the field of social work. However, we believe there to be an interdisciplinary commonality of purpose, technique and direction in supervision, and as such the following overview of the seminal explorations of the function, influence and thinking around supervision might act as a template in terms of establishing the tradition, logic, adequacy and development of practice.

Supervision as relationship

The usual understanding of supervision is that it involves someone, often a more senior individual, scrutinising the performance of a subordinate; examining functioning and perhaps some passing on of instructions and/or advice. However, in this chapter supervision will refer to a discipline deployed in the professional development and training of youth workers, much of which is relevant to other arenas including social work. It will also have relevance to other professions that deploy supervision as a developmental/assessment tool, including nursing, teaching, policing and the clergy.

Kadushin and Harkness (2002) draw attention to the interactional nature of supervision: there can be no supervisor without there being a supervisee. Hence supervision is a relationship, and one that is – at its best – 'co-operative, democratic, participatory, mutual, respectful, and open' (op. cit.: 22). Christian and Kitto (1987: 2) argue that supervision is a relationship between supervisor and supervisee, within which the supervisor's role is to 'enable' the supervisee. For them however this is not achieved via instruction or advice-giving. This is problematic, since while it leaves room for the supervisor to undertake the questioning; it effectively limits the potential within the supervisory situation in terms of critical analysis and theoretical content. At the same time it assumes there will be no need for advice or guidance from what is usually the senior professional in the relationship.

It is unclear what Kadushin and Harkness mean by the term 'relationship', its limits and possibilities. It would seem from experience and observation of supervisory encounters that they are more forms of association than relationship in the general understanding of the notion; the supervisor and supervisee usually meet and interact within relatively tightly prescribed professional parameters of behaviour and discourse. Any expectation of overtly intimate contact or straying outside the formal boundaries of practice cannot be countenanced (that would mean looking forward to the possibility of practice collapsing into a form of cosy comradeship or perhaps flirtatious friendship). In practice, the most efficacious supervisory encounter is active association between supervisor and supervisee. This might reflect youth work practice of youth workers that have been employed in both voluntary and statutory situations, and deployed within a wide range of contexts. These professionals work with individual and groups of young people and often base their practice in the purposeful associations they build with their clients, in everyday situations, using conversation and activities to generate ideas and perceptions that might be considered and reflected upon. Out of this it is hoped that clients will gain personal insight and learn about themselves, others and their world.

Professional judgement

The aim of supervision for Christian and Kitto is for the supervisee to 'think better' about their practice and, as a consequence 'work better'. However, how one might judge someone else is 'thinking better' is a moot point. According to Munro (2011: 41) social workers:

> . . . enable effective relationships, and are effective communicators, using appropriate skills. Using their professional judgement, they employ a range of interventions.

The development of professional judgement seems a more appropriate measure in terms of determining the relative success of supervision. The making of professional judgements defines the practitioner as something other than a neutral agent; they are obliged to make judgements. A judgement is different from an assumption or opinion; a judgement might be understood as an opinion based on evidence, the more evidence one has, the more secure one's judgement might be said to be. The more an opinion is made without evidence the more likely it might be to think of it as prejudice ('pre-judgement') or discrimination.

In terms of practice the worker is able to evidence professional judgement by demonstrating how and why they have chosen to do one thing rather than another. For instance, in supervision a youth worker recounted a particular instance of practice:

> The group came into the agency shouting and, what looked like play fighting, with each other. Others looked a bit intimidated, backing away from the group quite quickly. I chose not to immediately reproach them about this as when colleagues had done this before it had seemed to make matters worse. However, I had worked with a group previously that acted in much the same way and had noticed that engaging one or two of them in conversation had appeared to help the group acclimatise to the environment relatively straightforwardly. So, recognising Freda I commented how she had done her hair differently and how I thought it looked good . . .

Here you can see the worker, using a range of evidence drawn from their experience of practice, making her professional judgement; it is 'professional' because it is based on practice experience rather than personal bias. Her judgement might have been good, not so good or even poor (depending at least partly on the outcome) but she had nevertheless used judgement because she had drawn on evidence; her action was not based wholly on supposition, feelings and what is sometimes vaguely called 'instinct', but on judgement. This enabled her to make what might be considered an 'ethical choice': to take one course of action rather than another. This is something more than reflection, although reflection, and consideration, might be part of the process. It does not take much effort to understand how such situations can be examined in supervision to hone professional judgement. For Munro, more effective social workers are those who:

> *. . . are well prepared, knowledgeable about a child and family, articulate and confident in their evidence and confident in their professional judgements.*
>
> 2011: 92, 5.9

The use of evidence is directly related to making confident and useful professional judgements. However, Munro argues:

> *Currently, few social workers have detailed training in any evidenced method.*
>
> 2011: 55, 4.17

From this, together with her assertion that:

> *. . . such training is a long-term strategy. It is not enough to send someone on a two to three day course.*
>
> Ibid.

Munro is referring to specific approaches that have a positive impact, leading to a desired outcome.

This being the case, supervision needs to include critical discussion exploring evidenced methods, their character and potential, but also the need for workers to recognise, enhance and habituate the same as part of their own practice.

The Socratic Method

This model of supervision, common in youth work, reflects the attitude espoused by Christian and Kitto (1987). It effectively tasks the supervisor to work to produce a Socratic discourse, taking on a facilitative function, concentrating on the supervisee's description of their practice, encouraging reflection and learning via questioning.

It is claimed in much of the literature relating to this type of process that it is extremely appropriate to professionals who are commonly obliged to make and rely on their own judgement, via their perception of work-related situations and issues. This is thought to enhance the development of the capacity to take responsibility for their practice, its assessment and work to deal with the consequences of the same. However, there is little research to establish such assertions.

Claims that such routines are 'non-directive' are confusing, as the Socratic method is a means of instruction via a question and answer process that looks to elicit 'truths' from the questioned that the questioner considers to be implicitly known by all rational beings. The point of the Socratic method is not to be non-directive, but to guide (or manipulate) those questioned, by a particular form of direction, to uncover what is taken to be the knowledge inherent to them as rational beings. This being the case, the supervisor might not give information directly, but they do ask a series of questions. This line of enquiry results in the supervisee taking on desired ideas, techniques, perceptions, or in professional terms, reach a point at which they can be seen to understand and be complying with (if not totally in agreement) organisational principles, legislative or policy obligations, by answering the questions. This is often passed off as the achievement of 'deeper awareness' or defining the limits of their knowledge, both of which might be, but not necessarily, true.

This appears to be a very circuitous way of doing things just for the sake of appearing (rather than being) objective. It seems both more honest and more efficient for the supervisor to take responsibility for a more openly active role in the process, which will allow for clear expression and a critically, purposeful review of practice and an exploration motives, emotions and perspectives.

Overseers, teachers and innovators

The term 'supervisor' means literally 'overseer'. The traditional role of those who supervise has been generally taken to be ensuring that the quality of work being undertaken by others is of a standard. This could be considered an administrative role, but supervisors 'also had to be teachers and innovators' (Smith, 2005: 2). Christian and Kitto (1987) argue that supervision practice has grown from an ancient tradition, but that it emerged as a professional practice as a consequence of the psychoanalytic movement. Many authors distinguish between managerial and non-managerial supervision (for example, Stanners, 1995) although the differentiation is sometimes, in practice, hard to distinguish. However, for Munro, echoing recommendations by the Social Work Reform Board:

> . . . the two roles of managerial oversight and professional supervision need to be separated so that both are done properly. A division of career pathways at this point would also contribute to the establishment of a professional career pathway . . .
>
> 2011: 53–4, 4.12

Yarrow and Millwater (1997) make no distinction between supervision and mentoring in their study of an in-service professional development course for school teachers. Turner (2000: 232) discussing social work supervision and mentoring, suggests that the mentor's focus is the development and learning of the practitioner, whereas the supervisor's focus is much broader.

In this context, the mentor is appointed to support the practitioner's post-qualifying study and the supervisor is their line manager at work. Turner (2000: 239) considers mentoring for formal qualifications to be a role best separated from work supervision in order to maintain 'the need for impartiality and objectivity'. In voluntary sector organisations, staff team members undertaking study towards formal qualifications are likely to be appointed a tutor from the awarding institution with the role that Turner defines as mentoring.

Connexions personal advisors often work intensively with young people, in a manner analogous to those of some youth worker roles. Reviewing the supervision arrangements for Connexions personal advisors, Reid (2007: 59) found that the term had negative connotations for study participants, who preferred the phrase 'support and supervision'. Practitioners expressed a need for a restorative 'space to manage stress and avoid burn out' (Reid, 2007: 75). McMahon (2003) found limited evidence of supervision occurring in practice amongst Australian careers counsellors, despite considerable awareness and generally positive regard of supervision.

In addition to the available literature concerning work supervision in voluntary sector organisations, other writing considers supervision practice in related fields such as careers counselling. Perhaps amongst the most important examples of this is social work supervision theory. Some other 'people work' roles can be seen as being closer to social work than others – a housing support worker's job may have more similarities than a fitness instructor's role, for example. However, the literature on social work supervision provides a viable basis from which to explore the practice of supervision.

Legislative changes, such as the introduction of children's trust arrangements, have had the effect of standardising many working practices across statutory, voluntary and independent sectors. The common assessment framework for children might be understood as a good example of this, and some children's trusts introduced supervision standards for the children's workforce: these standards applied to all employing agencies. Indeed, statutory requirements for nursery funding insist on staff being supervised, and it is increasingly required for external quality standards such as 'Investors in People'.

Kadushin and Harkness (2002) provide a comprehensive definition of supervision in social work based on:

- The functions of supervision.
- Its objectives.
- The hierarchical position of supervisors.
- Supervision as an indirect service.
- The interactional process of supervision.

They propose that supervision has three overlapping functions, none of which can be discarded:

1. The administrative function of supervision aims to ensure adherence to, and effective implementation of, agency policies and procedures.
2. The educative function is focused on ensuring that the supervisee has sufficient skills and knowledge to do their job.
3. The supportive function aims to ensure worker morale and job satisfaction.

This arrangement is 'widely accepted by researchers of supervision' (Itzhaky and Hertzanu-Laty, 1999: 7).[3]

The short-term objectives of supervision are related to the three functions:

- Administrative supervision provides the work context that enables this effectiveness.
- Educational supervision aims to improve the worker's effectiveness.
- Supportive supervision aims to encourage and motivate the worker.

---

[3] By this definition supervision is a formalised continuation and concentration of things that happen in workplaces all the time, in the sense that colleagues support each other, practitioners learn through doing and reflecting, and they gain an understanding of agency administrative requirements through all sorts of everyday events, such as unintentional minor transgression of procedures for example.

In contrast to this emphasis, Stanners (1995) recommends that supervision within the 'caring' professions can be a process through which all participants gain support, guidance and insight; the overarching long-term objective of supervision being to ensure a good quality service to clients. Munro (2011: 50, 3.54) broadly agrees with this desired outcome. For her, the effort to apply relevant knowledge, to engage and motivate clients/families, requires skill that takes *time and critical reflection in supervision to develop.*

Noble and Irwin (2009: 347) suggest that supervision is most effective when the supervisee, 'engages in the process as a proactive participant interested in their own learning'. This might be thought of to equate to what Munro describes as 'critical and engaged supervision that supports the maintenance of a curious and robust practice'. (2011: 99)

A model for supervision

Many care, welfare and educational organisations have policy relating to staff supervision. These tend to note the benefits of regular supervision in terms of organisational effectiveness and ensuring good working relationships. For example, one policy document from an English YMCA states:

> *Supervision aids staff development . . . Most importantly it contributes to employee satisfaction . . . Every staff member must receive supervision at least once a month.*

Munro (2011), affirmed by Koehler and Harvey N. (2007) confirms this perspective:

> *. . . the availability and quality of supervision contributes to the quality of reasoning that social workers can achieve. Without time and encouragement to stop and review their work, social workers will operate at a primarily intuitive level with the associated risks of bias in their reasoning.*

The YMCA policy goes on to outline the areas that should usually be covered in the work supervision of staff:

- Responding to need.
- Checking that staff have the commitment, skills, knowledge and support they require to perform in their roles.
- Ensuring effectiveness, that staff understand their various responsibilities, and providing clear guidance on policies and procedures.
- Motivation, including giving constructive feedback and support.
- Discussion of training and development needs/opportunities.

Recently, the YMCA movement in England has developed a quality standards system, known as Insync. Local associations wishing to gain recognition under the Insync system must meet numerous specific requirements in relation to 'the key elements essential to the delivery of quality services to individuals and communities' (Milner and

Seaman, 2008: 4). There are several references to supervision in the standards, in sections covering:

- Whether staff are aware of professional boundaries.
- Ensuring staff have the commitment, skills, knowledge and support to provide high quality services.
- If staff and volunteers understand their responsibilities and what is expected of them.
- Clear guidelines about policies and procedures.
- Access to training and development opportunities for staff and volunteers to develop their potential.
- Whether staff have access to support and supervision, which includes the opportunity to discuss any concerns they have about their work.

Insync supervision standards together with the English YMCA policy on supervision come close to mirroring Munro's position that supervision is linked 'with practice, quality assurance and research' (2011: 57, 4.22). However, the approach to supervision that emerges also appears to include the administrative, educative and supportive functions of supervision, as defined by Kadushin and Harkness (2002). This said, there is little reference in the standards to the importance of developing relationships. The standards do mention developing and maintaining relationships through building trust and respecting confidences: this is in relation to ensuring a focus on clients, rather than being recognised as important throughout the organisation. In contrast, the Kampala Principles state that the mission of the YMCA implies imperatives such as:

> *To work for and maintain an environment in which relationships among people are characterised by love and understanding. To work for and maintain conditions, within the YMCA and in society, its organisations and institutions, which allow for honesty, depth and creativity.*
>
> Myles 1998, adopted in July 1973 at the World Council of YMCAs in Kampala

Hence, the language with which the YMCA describes its priorities seems to have moved from a strong emphasis on interpersonal/interactional considerations to a focus on demonstrating value, achieving objectives, clarity of purpose, and promoting individual growth and development. This is something that has become ubiquitous across the educational and care environment over the last decade.

With regard to clients, Insync does contain a section on involvement, which considers the participation and engagement of clients – particularly in the management and governance of YMCA associations. This section asks the question:

> *Do your methods of working together build interpersonal relationships based on mutual respect and a spirit of acceptance?*
>
> Milner and Seaman, 2008: 33

So, the Insync standards do recognise to some degree the importance of a relational approach to working with clients, although this is centred on the methods being used.

This model and the principles and attitudes encompassed by it, reflect a definite shift in the aims and looked-for product of supervision, moving away from a therapeutic or treatment emphasis (making people and practice 'better') towards are more pragmatic, managerial ethos, or as some might argue, mechanistic function.

Kadushin and Harkness (2002) endorse the three-tier model of social work organisations, according to which supervisors operate at the managerial level. At the institutional or administrative level, policies are set, programmes are planned and external networks are engaged to further the strategic direction of the organisation. At the managerial level supervisors implement programmes, focussing on the work environment and the tasks at hand. Supervisors therefore act as an organisational bridge between senior managers and front-line workers. At the technical level, workers provide a direct service to the organisation's clients.

YMCAs in England deliver a diverse range of services, crossing a number of disciplinary boundaries. Although wider in scope than many statutory social work situations, the general focus is on meeting the needs of individuals, groups and communities within society. Stanners (1995) notes that there is rarely a career structure within voluntary sector organisations. Hence, in terms of the YMCA, like many other large non-statutory organisations, the three-tier model of organisations – with a neat separation of the ambassadorial and strategic functions of the administration from the concerns with effectiveness and efficiency of management – is rarely realised in practice. Furthermore, line managers may supervise staff team members from different teams and departments: these staff team members may be undertaking quite different areas of work – in supported housing or sports, for example. A senior manager is unlikely to have a background or qualifications in all the functional areas within which they will supervise staff team members.

YMCAs, typical of many voluntary organisations, differ in size and activities undertaken, and the supportive, administrative and educative functions of supervision are relevant beyond the supervision of front-line workers. The long-term objective in the Kadushin and Harkness model of providing a higher quality service to clients also fails to distinguish managerial supervision of front-line workers from the supervision of managers.

The line manager as supervisor

Christian and Kitto (1987) suggest a limitation to supervision where the supervisor is also the line manager, based on their treatment of roles and responsibilities. They suggest that the supervisor ideally has the freedom to allow the worker to take full responsibility for the work – and to therefore experience the consequences of any decisions made, including conclusions drawn from the supervision process. A line manager, however, may need to prohibit a course of action owing to agency guidelines, for example. Christian and Kitto acknowledge that this may not matter much in practice, especially where the worker is competent.

However, non-managerial supervisors are often paid by the organisations that employ them, although sometimes supervisees might pay fees. But whatever the case, the supervisor's functioning will be influenced by the context, rules, regulations, traditions and customs of the supervisee's employing organisation; the limits and possibilities of supervisee action are mediated by the same. Supervisors also need to work within/be mindful of legal frameworks of any professional situation and if possible advise, when necessary, supervisees of their position in law. Failing to do this would be at least malpractice, but also supervisors might, in some instances where issues are traced back to the supervisory situation, be taken as at least partly culpable if the person whom they supervise falls foul of the law relating to their practice. With this in mind, the unvarying 'sounding board' or inveterate questioning asking supervisor walks a risky line.

Given the above, supervisors (even those giving their time freely) are required to understand, consider and generally work for the supervisee to effectively forward/ enhance agency guidelines, aims, objectives, purpose, ethos, philosophy and culture, as well as be diligent with regard to how the law relates to their supervisee's practice. If this were not the case they might find themselves working with supervisees to the detriment of the latter's organisation and so their own employment/professional prospects. As such it can be seen that the distinction between non-managerial and managerial supervision is often blurred and sometimes spurious.

This said, Hess (1987) describes a situation wherein the organisational status of a line manager inhibited honest reflection in supervision. The line manager reported that employees whom he supervised understood that he was able to separate what he had heard in supervision from his decisions about pay rises. In contrast, his employee-supervisees were clear that they carefully censored the material they brought to supervision so that their merit evaluation would not be put at risk (Hess 1987: 253–4).

Hence it is possible that the candid exploration of work–related issues is inhibited in supervision conducted by line managers or any supervision funded from organisational finance, because supervisees, not wanting to appear incompetent to the person who may determine matters such as their pay rises, promotion or even access to perks. However, in many voluntary organisations terms and conditions are not directly controlled by line managers.

For all this, supervisees may worry that formal appraisals might be affected by admitting uncertainty or inadequacy in the course of supervision. It should also be pointed out that it is not unusual for non-managerial supervisors to be required to produce progress reports or assessments of the supervisees they are paid to work with and as such be in much the same position as the managerial supervisors whom Hess (1987) refers to.

A tense association?

Kadushin conducted a survey of social work supervisors and their supervisees in 1974, focusing on their perceptions of the supervisory association. The results suggested that supervisees placed a deal of stress on their supervisors' positional power. However, the supervisors were inclined to perceive that their more expansive expertise was the basis of what influence they had. What was consistently evident was ambivalence in terms of expectations about and the general stance of supervision. Supervisees expressed an aspiration for supervisors to work with them to reflect on and consider their practice, but criticised constraining, authoritarian and controlling supervisors. However, somewhat contradictorily, they also expressed a want to be instructed on how to best work with their clients. Correspondingly supervisors, although expressing a wish to support the development of supervisees, including their ability to take on professional responsibility, while seeing their function as consultative/educative, in practice gave over an inordinate amount of time in supervision to advising supervisees about procedure and policy. Mirroring and extending Kadushin's research, Cherniss and Egnatios (1978) and Gardiner (1989) came up with similar conclusions.

Collectively the above research demonstrates supervisor/supervisee expectations of, and attitudes to supervision might be in tension if not altogether conflictual. But, Gardiner (1989) apart, generally research into supervision provides only a very limited view of approaches, feelings and thinking about supervision, at specific times, in particular situations and places. However, Gardiner, deploying case studies, demonstrated something of how conceptions about and attitudes towards supervision altered over time as supervisees became more self-assured as learners. This might be understood to suggest the significance of the supervisor looking to gain awareness of the supervisees' development path and learning direction, essentially working with them to support advances in knowledge and skills, together with personal and professional growth. Less experienced/skilled supervisors who see their role as basically or chiefly instruction might have found this endeavour more demanding.

A service to clients

For Kadushin and Harkness (2002) supervision is an indirect service to clients: supervisors improve the service that clients receive through developing the competence and skills of an organisation's front-line workers. However, this is quite an idealistic position in that it presupposes that, say, not-for-profit organisations will have exactly the same attitudes in this respect to commercial oriented situations . Supervision can be oriented as much to efficiency or sufficiency as effectiveness. Kadushin and Harkness note that there is limited empirical evidence for the model that they present, with studies suggesting that supervisors in practice differ widely in the tasks that they undertake as part of the supervision process.

Smith (2005) notes that Kadushin and Harkness' model tends to envisage the worker as in some way lacking, needing the supervisor to correct deficiencies: he attributes this to their approach to management, which emphasises the responsibility of the supervisors to the agency for the quality/effectiveness of their staff. He recommends an approach to management that stresses conversation and a concern for fostering an environment[4] in which workers can take responsibility for their own actions (Smith

---

[4]The concept of 'fostering an environment' may not imply the lack of a shared understanding that the supervisee is able to take decisions and exercise responsibility. The fostering activity might only impinge where the supervisee is not already taking responsibility and this is not recognised by the supervisor. However, to foster is to 'look after'.

2005: 4) although how much the 'fostering' activity on the part of the supervisor might contradictorily impinge on the responsibility-taking of the supervisee is not considered.

Supervision in youth work

What is arguably seen as the seminal piece of research in the supervision field was undertaken by Joan Tash (1967). Tash was involved with training youth workers to supervise. However, nearly half a century later, while the advantages of supervision are consistently championed by most practitioners in the youth work field, provision is at best erratic and agreement about its purpose and delivery differentiated. In the main supervision is used by managers, generally as a means by which those they are responsible for might make reports about their functioning and provide a vista for checking activity. This is quite dissimilar to the developmental process Tash took supervision to be.

Following on from Tash it is often argued that supervision is an exceptionally relevant practice in terms of the professional development for youth workers because it looks to educate via the supervisory encounter, which is used to promote reflection on experience. This process is claimed to mirror youth work practice with young people. This analogical approach has been claimed to offer the potential for the professional to learn by way of the process and the content of supervision.

The character of youth work practice often obliges its practitioners to be able to respond swiftly, sometimes spontaneously, to situations and over contexts. They need to make the most of learning opportunities for their clients as and when they are presented, while making sure that the primary aims of their work, the care, welfare and protection of young people, are attended to. It is not unusual for professionals' day-to-day role and function in this sphere to lack clear, formal structure, outside of the expectation of a duty of care.

Given this situation many of the proponents of supervision in the youth work arena assert that practitioners need to develop the ability to 'reflect-in-and-on-action'. The capacity to reflect on practice generally, both pre and post practice is taken to be pivotal to best practice. This being the case this reflective activity is seen as more necessary than merely desirable because of the need to assess the effectiveness (or otherwise) of work done, and to comprehend the emotional impact of the youth work role on the worker. It is also meant to be a guide to both current and future practice.

But despite this, many youth workers are ambivalent about supervision, while the level of research into supervision within the field is negligible in terms of quality and quantity. At the same time, given the pressures of youth work, both in terms of the situation presented by its clientele and doubts about the future of the profession, it appears imperative that youth workers find relevant ways to develop good practice, which can be seen to be as pertinent to the modern world and the social, organisational and political expectations of their function.

It has been claimed that the best supervisory practice can emancipate and enlarge the experience of practitioners (Dewey's notion of education, 1933: 240) and their clients. It is thought to facilitate ways and means of working with clients to produce a similar type of emancipation on the latter's part. However, it is hard for those of us intimately involved with and in youth work to point to any viable, sizable or widespread 'emancipation' of those we work with and amongst, while our own professional position, far from taking an emancipatory path, seems more confined and restricted by bureaucracy and managerial surveillance than at any point since youth work became a role recognised and offered on a national scale after the Second World War. The economic position and outlook of those groups focused on or targeted by youth work have changed negligibly in relative terms over the last half-century. This might of course be because of the lack of wide-spread supervision. However, it may also be more related to macro-socioeconomic conditions and the inherently exploitative character of societies driven and guided by capitalist enterprise, the ethos and purpose of which will be reflected in and maintained by its institutions. The latter include education and welfare provision, within which youth workers and their supervisors are employed. While third sector youth work or socially educative agencies do not of themselves maintain the fabric of globalised capitalism, the capitalist character of our society is reflected across its social infrastructure. Everyone in youth work needs to function along generalised best practice guidelines, formalised policy and legislation. While some youth workers and some youth work agencies might want or even believe they operate 'outside the system', it is unclear quite where the outside is. Maverick youth work agencies might be considered to be as rare as a deviant iron filing that moves away from the magnetic attraction that pulls all other iron filings towards it.

The supervisory paradigm

Over the last decade there has been very little added to the canon of supervision theory. To a great extent the supervisory paradigm has been reiterated and often straightforwardly repeated by writers and academics. However, there is a discernable conceptual framework that many have tried to formulate as the educational theory which underpins the subject. This depicts supervision as essentially being premised on learning from experience. This begs the question of course as to how anything can be learnt outside of experience, but at root the process of supervision might be thought of as looking at how something happens, asking why it happened in a particular way and how things might have been different. Hence it can become as much an exercise in speculation and imagination (or fantasy and dreaming) as anything else. But why should this be of importance in terms of practice development?

Dewey (1925: 244) has it that experience does not routinely result in learning. Insight is obtainable by examination or interrogation of experience, looking at meaning and what we have understood from our experience. For him '. . . events are present and operative anyway; what concerns us is their meaning.

This, according to Dewey, is the way we might generate knowledge in response to experience. This is articulated and built via reflection and discussion:

. . . meanings arise in the process of interaction between people . . .
Bullough, Knowles and Crow, 1991: 3

This can be seen to differ from the perception of education that posits the teacher as the holder of knowledge (although it is debatable how far, if at all, this idea of the teacher as the font of all wisdom is bought into by educationalists over the last two decades). It is argued that the teaching or learning arising out of supervision happens within the facilitative process that it is. For Arnett (1986) supervision advocates insist that the process is not instructional. According to him it encourages active participation on the part of learners. While this might be understood as a sort of instructional process in itself (one must actively participate) Arnett sees it as the learner defining the substance and trajectory of their own learning.

For Freire (1996) this type of education is fundamentally liberating (although, as stated above, it might not be totally emancipatory). In much the same vein, Rogers (1983) argued that people develop their freedom to learn when they chose their own personal path, finding learning resources for themselves, while formulating their own problems, deciding their own course of action and finally living with the result of these choices (Rogers, 1969, quoted in Gardiner, 1989: 56).

Freire and Rogers share a desire to reduce the hierarchy between educator and student, and to move away from a content-centred approach to education. The key difference in their theories surrounds their concepts of selfhood.

Rogers perceives people as being individually autonomous and free to pursue an innate actualising tendency: he had 'an individualistic or egocentric concept of personhood' (O'Hara, 1989: 17). While Rogers and Freire both value authenticity, for Rogers this means individual freedom to interpret the world, while for Freire it is to be free of the distortions of interpretation created by the powerful for the purpose of oppressing the powerless (O'Hara, 1989).

While it might be gathered from the above that supervision can be a 'zone of learning freedom', in actuality the supervisee is relatively limited in this respect, given professional, policy, organisational and legislative considerations. However, at the same time, this emphasis on learner autonomy logically problematises the presence of the supervisor, who seems to have a sort of 'inactive active' role. The ambition seems to be to present a totally detached confidant, who unflinchingly is both present in, yet absent from, the learning event. The character of Socratic Method deployed apart, this borders on a sort of mystic role of a non-intrusive, yet essentially guiding influence.

For all this, a number of writers have identified stages in the process of learning from experience, including Dewey (1933), Kolb (1982) and Boud, Keogh and Walker (1985). However, within the literature surrounding supervision there is a shared theoretical perspective that coagulates around an interaction between experience, reflection on/consideration of the same, and the development of novel insights and understanding that alter the perception of and reactions to subsequent experience.

For Revans (1980) and Schon (1983) professionals should purposefully and constantly undertake endeavour of this type in order that they might maintain effective practice within contexts that are uncertain, complex and sometimes conflictual. In the process the professional becomes self educating, taking on the role of a researcher into their own practice (Schon, 1983: 17; 299). Supervision might be thought of as the formalisation of this method; a sort of structured navel gazing – by way of focused discussion, alongside the supervisor, the professional revisits, via reflection, practice experience, looking to discern and define meaning from the same.

The learning process

Since the mid-1960s there has been a quest to understand the learning processes of students in Higher Education. This started with the likes of Hudson (1966) Perry (1970) Pask (1976) Marton and Saljo (1976) Fransson (1977) and Witkin (1977). Entwistle (1977) argued that this research provided parallel findings, around the impact of students adopting various approaches and styles of thought, on the quality of learning, how this related to the stage of learning development that students occupied and to their understanding of what was to be learnt. While there were slight differences in the manner in which their findings were presented, these writers commonly identified students with the propensity to have a dependent, reproductive approach to learning. However, others tended to work to understand deeper meaning and linkages between concepts 'the signified more than the sign' (Entwistle, 1977).

For Laurillard (1978) student attitudes to learning are affected by their awareness of what they need to do or achieve relative to the learning task, their level of understanding of the methods of teaching, assessment and the requirement on them to take an apposite approach to learning.

Most of the studies identified qualitative variations in the learning of students. This appeared to be influenced by which conceptual approach they adopted. What Marton and Saljo (1976) refer to as 'Deep level processors' appeared capable of creating and blending ideas to formulate their own perspective (a movement from the dialogical to dialectical thinking). These individuals seemed to have been versatile thinkers (Entwistle, 1977); apparently they adopted a 'surface level' approach if they understood this to be fitting to the requirements of any particular learning task. However, surface level processors experienced problems making moves away from a dependence on reproductive thinking.

In the main this literature applied itself to student learning from academic requirements, but it is relevant to the exploration of the effects and outcomes of supervision, as the practice claims to facilitate development of deeper understanding, that in turn is said to enable practitioners to critically examine their role and actions, independent of other influences or perspectives.

Relying heavily on Swedish research, Gardiner (1989) examining teaching and learning in supervision of student social workers, found that, using case studies, supervisors often effectively concentrated on a paradigm of instruction. This, seemingly inadvertently, necessarily clove to surface-reproductive learning. For Gardiner, working with social work students, a move to a more illuminated paradigm was needed to facilitate deeper, more independent forms of thinking. When this did happen, Gardiner found that students shifted from what he saw as a surface level engagement with facts and method, to a much more active quest to derive meaning from experience: 'meta-learning'. According to Gardiner this was the ability to examine the process of learning, while using and assessing diverse tactics in a variety of undertakings and situations. This feels convincing, but without sure methods by which the relative extent of the process of learning might be measured, it is hard to establish how far Gardiner was seeing what he wanted to see, looking, albeit unconsciously, to promote supervision practice.

This possibility is sustained by research into supervision of counsellors (Payne, Winter and Bell, 1972) that to some extent contradicted Gardiner's position, suggesting that students experienced more successful learning outcomes from instructional/didactic supervision approaches. However, the researchers appeared to be mostly preoccupied with the way in which counsellors gained a grasp on functional procedures, while Gardiner was essentially looking at the development of autonomous, deeper-level assessment/consideration of practice.

The value of the learning style and strategy of research in terms of looking at how we might understand the experience of learners/supervisees has its limitations. The terms imply a level of premeditated preference, but do we deliberately make such choices in terms of our approach to learning; do we have a particular and conscious way obtaining insight? Maybe we do if we understand an undertaking as encouraging a specific approach (for instance, committing the means of wiring a plug to memory or learning the Highway Code). However, the theories of style and strategy might be thought of as problematical as they are inclined to fail to address the sometimes illogical considerations that can impact our attitudes to learning.

Calling on psychoanalytic ideas and perspectives Saltzberger-Wittenberg, Henry and Osborne (1983) looked at the influence of the not altogether conscious, emotionally founded effects on learning. For them it is not uncommon for adult students to transfer anxiety and childhood experiences of school or family into new learning circumstances. They argue that the main effect in terms of our liberty to learn deeply is the intensity of anxiety that the teaching/learning context provokes, and the level of endeavour we exert to reduce the resulting distress. As such, learners feeling relatively high anxiety are liable to be limited to surface-reproductive thinking and rely on teachers to provide answers/solutions. This is posited as an effort to decrease anxiety about ambiguity.

Research into learning styles and strategies has recognised a connection between learner anxiety and dependence. For instance, Entwistle (1977) and Fransson (1977) argue that students provoked by concern about failure have an inclination to grab at answers and were reluctant to make attempts at expressing their own points of view or to be critical of received wisdom because of fear about being wrong. Taking this further, Saltzberger, Wittenberg et al. (1983: 5) maintain that educators should equip students to recognise their anxieties in order that they might be subject to '. . . the more mature part of the personality . . .' For them, this would mean that fears could be more rationally considered and so managed. Problematic emotions can potentially be processed into learning rather than remaining a possible blockage to the same. The quality of the association between the teacher and the learner is understood as crucial in this situation. The teacher who shows themselves to be able to contain and consider student distress, while desisting from the temptation to instruct or give advice, is thought to be able to facilitate and/or mirror the development of like capacities within the student '. . . to internalise a thinking person' (p60).

However, not giving answers to a person desperate to find an answer might be both challenging and frustrating for all concerned. Teachers carry a cultural expectation of being able to respond to questions, even if only in a way that inspires more questioning. A simplistic refusal to provide often necessary advice, or to instruct when appropriate, might well be confusing and even fuel the rejection of education. For example, think of yourself waiting at a bus stop. You look at the timetable to find out when the next bus is due, but when you look at your watch you find it has stopped. There is another person waiting at the bus stop with you and you see they have a watch, so you ask them for the right time. If would be both frustrating and disappointing if your potential fellow passenger, rather than telling you the time, asked you; 'What do you think the time is?'

Rogers (1983) like Maslow (1968) saw the amalgam of the cognitive and emotional as being crucial to the development of independent, deep-level learning, and an aspect of movement to realising oneself as a fully operative, self-actualised individual. This is resonant of Dewey (1933) for whom extracting meaning and comprehension of situations and circumstances from emotional cues, clues and expressions was as an imperative component of learning. These ideas appear to have relevance for supervision, perhaps more so if we could distinguish what 'deep-learning' might be and if it could be relative in terms of individuals and contexts.

Mental and emotional stabilising

The potential supervision has to mentally and emotionally situate supervisees within the tumult of practice has been described by Mistry and Brown (1997) who see it as allowing thought about the inherent perplexities and quandaries. For all this, Gardiner (1989) abhors what he sees as the seepage of such psychoanalytic notions into supervision, arguing that this muddles supervision with therapy. However, it is possible to see that there is reciprocity between the cognitive functions relevant to learning and our emotions. This said, psychoanalytic language and thinking transferred into the context of supervision, by those without appropriate training, support or qualification – and who might have relatively little experience of the use and consequences of the same – does place the supervisory association at risk. At the same time it might expose the supervisor and the supervisee to a whole realm of corollaries, not least the difficulties of projection, transference, counter-transference[5] and direct confrontation with the unconscious. If one gives any credence to the supposed power of the psychoanalytical encounter it is not hard to imagine its potential to confuse and damage the untrained, ill-prepared and dabbling experimentalist. By association the clients of the supervisee are placed in jeopardy, particularly if the supervisee mirrors the supervisory practice in their work with others (a likelihood often cited in the literature).

Rosenblatt and Mayer (1975) and earlier Kadushin (1968) have argued that this type of confusion within the supervisory encounter is likely to happen when there is ambiguity about the aim of supervision and the function of the supervisor. But if psychoanalytic approaches, that can and are encompassed into wider psycho-therapeutic practice, are deployed it is clear that this will almost inevitably invite disorientation as both the supervisor and the supervisee roll down the tram line being laid to the unconscious. While some might argue that psychoanalytic theory can elucidate learning, opening up the roots of anxiety that might be influencing the supervisee, it has to be at least doubtful that the amateur psychoanalyst can consistently control the trajectory of the therapeutic journey to this extent. It also seems to risk them finding themselves and their supervisee travelling along tangents that not only might have little relevance to practice, but introduce a whole range of complexities to the professional association that neither side may be able to predict, manage or navigate.

For all this, any belief in psychoanalysis is reliant on the faith that it is premised on the interpretation of unconscious motives, which will encompass imaginings, dreams and fantasy, albeit extrapolated from evidence of observable behaviour. Such trawling of the depths beneath straightforward reality seems intrinsically unsuitable to the project of supervision, set as it is in the concrete practice situation. It is perhaps fair to say that psychoanalytical method is about as suitable to supervision as it would be to the practice of the legal advocate or barrister, in that both roles function to examine definite evidence. While some of the same may arise from or involve feelings, which might have roots in childhood experience or personal neurosis, neither the courtroom nor the supervisory encounter seem particularly appropriate places for Freudian, Adlerian or Jungian (etc.) expeditions into the hardly fathomable dominion of the unconscious. The pressures of time, the lack of personnel, support and expertise

---

[5]**Transference** might be understood as a sort of time machine affect. If one is reminded of something from one's past by something said or done by another, psychoanalytic theory has it that this can transfer an emotional/psychological need or disposition into the present. For instance, I might relive a relationship with my father with my supervisor, trying perhaps to gain love or avoid punishment.

Projection might be thought of as a form of transference. It is the process of moving ones own feelings, emotions or motivations into another person, without realising this reaction is really more about one's own situation than the actions of the other person.

Supervisors, like health care professionals or psychotherapists, can get involved in **counter-transference**. Basically this is again the operation of the emotional time machine. In the supervisory encounter it would be a situation the supervisor can find themselves in reacting to the transference of the supervisee; a counter-reaction. A supervisor might believe they are falling in love with their supervisee following a supervisee transferring feelings of love into the supervisory relationship.

together can incite, at best, poor or second rate psychoanalytic practice and at worse supervisory malpractice.

Playing the game

The influence on learning caused by anxiety was looked at by Kadushin (1968: 23). Deploying the idea of 'game playing' in supervision, he saw social work students and their supervisors colluding in '. . . defensive adjustments to the threats and anxieties' in the supervisory encounter. For Kadushin, the chief tactic used by supervisees was to move the concentration in supervision away from practice via the reframing of the supervisory association; for instance, acting in such a manner to motivate supervisors to act as experts or adopt the role of friend, therapist, parent, assistant etc. Kadushin argued that supervisors not only effectively collaborated with diversions of this type; they, not uncommonly, instigated the same. He found that while such games had the potential for short-lived respite from anxiety, they ultimately prevented the supervisee from using the supervisory encounter to facilitate professional development. For Kadushin the mutual indulgence in these 'games' meant the supervisee lost by winning (p32).

While he claims that such behaviour is clearly distinguishable and well established, Kadushin seems to have formulated this perspective not from any rigorous research model, but merely on the basis of his own experience of training and supervising social workers. He does not provide a series of rigorous case studies and control groups to support his declarations about the defensive processes he claims take place within supervision. However, the logic of his point demonstrates the problems clearly. Perhaps this is the final nail in the coffin of transferring psychoanalytic musings into supervision; ultimately it seems the creaking cart drags the wheezing horse over a precipice of allusion, speculation and the potential for imagination to overtake the need to evidence practice claims and research.

Interpersonal or reciprocal influence

In the process of a more general investigation of stressful practice situations, looking at supervision from the perspective of social work supervisees, Rosenblatt and Mayer (1975) indentified clear dissatisfaction with supervisors as being a basis of stress in approximately 20 per cent of respondents. Certain examples of obstructive supervisor performance were isolated and the tactics students formulated in the face of the same. In the main this was the avoidance of revealing significant details relating to their work. Some accounts saw the outcome of this being a loss practice confidence. Student autobiography of supervision was used. Peer interviews were deployed to follow this up wherein the autobiographies were explored. Examination of perceptions revealed a high level of internal consistency between respondents. But the perspective that becomes apparent failed to illustrate the extent of a possible reciprocal impact in terms of supervisor/supervisee interaction, as the research only addressed student percep-tions of their supervisory association.

Holloway (1982) looked at reciprocal influences, discerning sequential configurations of verbal performance in the supervisory interaction. It appeared that patterns of reciprocal influence developed over time via a succession of transactions. Holloway concluded that particular supervisor behaviour regularly engendered like reactions from supervisees. For instance, after supervisors made suggestions or passed opinions, supervisees were liable to fail to articulate their own ideas or perspectives. If the supervisor questioned the supervisees' ideas or opinions directly this often evoked silence. However, if supervisors encouraged discussion of the supervisee's personal experiences, feelings or thoughts, this often gave rise to what Holloway saw as '... positive social emotional behaviour'. This said, Holloway made use of a very small sample of a specific professional group and his work was never replicated. Like most of the research into supervision no control groups were established by which comparative and perhaps informative findings might have been generated.

Interpersonal influence within supervision was also examined by Heppner and Handley (1981). Their focus was on the supervisee's perceptions of the trustworthiness, attractiveness and expertise of the supervisor. They found that the methodology they employed was unable to fathom the density of processes within supervision. They also concluded that other variables required consideration. For all this, Heppner and Handley managed to demonstrate a level of relationship between these factors and the satisfaction of supervisee experience of supervision.

Tash (1967) undertook two years of research during which she trained ten senior workers as supervisors. The supervisees of these supervisors were newly qualified practitioners. Tash used supervision with herself (she acted as the supervisor of the supervisors) as the primary training method. Recurrently examining her own recordings and findings with subjects, she generated an evaluation of the research, which provided information about her supervision, together with the trainee supervisors' impression of how their practice was influenced. For instance, the trainee supervisors were said to have steadily shifted from what Tash identified as dependence on her to become autonomous and reflective in terms of their professional activity (no consistent measure was applied and as there was no control group, no comparative critique was generated).

Tash concluded that the trainees found supervision sustaining and affirming both on personal and professional levels (this conclusion was based on personal opinion, judgement and anecdotal evidence). The research also made the point that the trainees felt confident about discussing their practice-related vulnerabilities as they understood such disclosure would not be revealed outside supervision or held against them within the same. However, the latter appears to be more like secrecy than confidentiality, while the former might be hard to affirm (no 'standard' measure of confidence was applied). These ethical considerations were not addressed in any adequate way.

For Tash, the trainees began to discern meaning in their practice and as a consequence were more capable of explicating the same to others. It is unclear if these conclusions were ever checked out with the trainee's supervisees over time, together with other workers or clients. As such, they could represent reliable extrapolations, mere imaginings, fantasy, the product of memory lapses or mistakes of perception or understanding. Tash also claimed that trainees were able to identify their own theories in use. Once more the reader is left to speculate on the usefulness or otherwise of the same; given my theory is useful, how can I be a reliable/subjective witness to this given the problems with 'feelings of certitude' that Munro (2011) has identified (see Introduction)?

Smaller pieces of research have looked at the influence of supervision on practice. For example, Kadushin (1976) cites Henry, Sims and Spray (1971) and others. Olmstead and Christensen (1973) found that respondents (social workers) rated supervision the most important facet in terms of professional development. They also expressed the belief that it had a positive effect on their levels of competence and job satisfaction. In keeping with the tradition of research into supervision there was no means of affirming any of these claims beyond supervisee declarations and anecdotes. Kadushin (like many writers on the subject) fails to put forward any solid critique of this research, but, for the most part, appears to deploy it to support his position about supervision that is an essential element of good practice in social work.

Biasco and Redfering (1976) found that just over three quarters (76 per cent) of clients taking part in group counselling delivered by a supervised counsellor felt that their experience had been helpful. This compared with under half (42 per cent) in the groups where the counselling was delivered by unsupervised practitioners. The supervised counsellors reported greater personal growth and learning during the research and expressed more concern about professional ethics (i.e. confidentiality). This group by and large tended to more fully evaluate their practice and were more positive about their functioning than the unsupervised counsellors. However, how can it be ascertained that supervision was the crucial influence? Any number of other considerations may have added to or been responsible for the level of client satisfaction. At the same time it is hard to tell if client satisfaction can be taken as an indicator of counselling success. Clients can be satisfied because they have had an 'easy' session or have managed to manipulate the counsellor. However, the research is of interest as it is innovative, in terms of research into supervision, as it sought to make a direct connection between supervision and client satisfaction.

Lanning (1971) concluded that supervisees in counselling modelled their relationships with their clients on their perceived relationship with their supervisor. This is hardly surprising as they would need to model their approach on something and, in that they were attending supervision, logic might suggest that this would have some, perhaps significant, impact.

In much the same vein, Pierce and Schauble (1970) argued that the supervisees of more empathetic supervisors, who provided noticeably high levels of regard, genuineness and 'concreteness', would more probably extend a similar approach to their clients than those whose supervisors were less empathetic etc. Doubt about how one might effectively measure or establish relative empathy, regard, genuineness or 'concreteness', and how individuals from different backgrounds and varying age and gender groups might perceive the same, probably leads Pierce and Schauble's research into something of a cul-de-sac.

However, Karr and Geist's (1977) research more or less supported Pierce and

Schauble (1970) while Austin and Altekruse (1972) suggested that supervisees in receipt of 'non-restrictive' supervision had more understanding of their clients than those on the receiving end of 'restrictive supervisors'.

On the basis of the above research one might tentatively suggest that the approach that supervisors use in supervision will have an impact on their supervisees associations with their clients. This would confirm Saltzberger-Wittenberg et. al. (1983: 60) who wrote about the internalisation of the supervisor by the supervisee. This position was effectively challenged by Deming (1980) who tested the supposition that more effective practice would be delivered by more 'self-actualised' practitioners. Deming concluded that counselling students' levels of self-actualisation were unaffected by the level of self-actualisation of their supervisors. However, self-actualisation, being defined by Deming as an ideal of psychological well-being, provides a very fuzzy measurement tool on which no steadfast conclusions can be based.

Overall, it is hard to have any conviction about the proposed influence of supervisor approach on supervisees, given the relatively weak research frameworks deployed by writers in this area. There also appears to be a lack of recent research into the supervision process, Gardiner (1989) being the latest study of any substance identified. Most research has been in the context of social work or counselling, with only one study located in youth work. However, it seems to make a case for a more straightforward, uncluttered and generic form of supervision practice. Something of this type can be identified in Munro (2011: 50, 3.52). For her, the conventional understanding of the front line, caseload-carrying worker, supported by moderate level of supervision requires revision. She sees the position of the junior doctor as a useful model, having '. . . access to consultation and ongoing training from more experienced colleagues and can contact a specialist when dealing with novel problems'.

Although Munro is clear that:

> Managers will need to be provided with support and training that provides them with the supervision skills that enable reflective practice, skills that enable, encourage and question the evidence base on which their social workers are practising.

p. 52, 4.9

Conclusion

Many of the social work and counselling researchers draw almost exclusively on literature and research within their own fields. This exclusivity may limit their contribution to the development of a generic, transferable understanding of the central elements of the supervision process per se. Kitto (1993) sees this tendency as fragmenting supervision into different types, for example, social work supervision, counselling supervision, managerial supervision, non-managerial supervision, etc. For her this has lead to a lack of clarity about the essential purpose and functions of supervision and about the role of the supervisor. However, a number of general themes emerge from the research:

- Supervisees' approaches to supervision is likely to be influenced by their stage of development as learners, their conception of the learning task, and their ability to manage their anxiety.
- If supervision is to encourage movement toward deeper, more critical thinking, then the nature of the supervisory process and association might facilitate this.
- Both supervisors and supervisees may be ambivalent in their attitudes and expectations, torn between the desire for dependent, instructional supervisory relationships and those which foster supervisee autonomy.
- Supervision doesn't exist in a vacuum but operates in response to the prevailing operational and organisational environment.

The complexity of the supervision process is strongly indicated, not surprisingly, since supervision takes place through an association between individuals. This means that there will always be at least two different perceptions of the situation in operation at any time, with the supervisee and the supervisor constantly adjusting their behaviour according to their perceptions of each other (see Goffman, 1959). In order to understand such processes research needs to seek out the meaning which participants attach to their experience of supervision and this involves accessing feelings, attitudes and values. The need to deploy qualitative methodologies over longer timescales is therefore indicated.

However, with the exception of Tash (1967), Rosenblatt and Mayer (1975) and Gardiner (1989) research into supervision appears to employ short-term methods, using pre-set response categories. These have tended to skim the surface and limit the range of possible responses. Indeed, questions have been raised about the reliability of some of the research into the supervision of counsellors. Hansen, Pound and Petro (1976) reviewing five years of research in that field, concluded that in general it lacked rigour and generalisability. Sample sizes were inadequate and there was a lack of specificity in variable definition. They therefore urge caution in the interpretation or application of its results. All these failings seem to be applicable throughout the literature relating to supervision. That said, while lack of generalisability and apprehension about the identification of variables might concern the researcher working from a nomothetic perspective, from an ideographic perspective, the meanings and understandings presented in more rigorous small-scale studies may present convincing findings and resonate with the professional experience.

Ultimately, despite Muncie's position that supervision is integral to social work practice and not an add-on, perhaps Ash is all too often proved correct in his contention:

> *Like so many 'essentials' to good practice, supervision frequently happens more in the intention than in the reality.*

Ash in Pritchard, 1997: 20

References

Arnett, R. (1986) *Communication and Community: Implications of Martin Buber Dialogue*. Illinois University Press.

Austin, B. and Altekruse, M.K. (1972) The Effect of Group Supervision Roles on Practicum Students' Interview Behaviour. In *Counselor Education and Supervision*, 12: 1, 63–8.

Biasco, F. and Redfering, D.L. (1976) Effects of Counsellor Supervision on Group Counselling: Clients' Perceived Outcomes. In *Counselor Education and Supervision*, 15: 3, 216–20.

Binfield, C. (1994) *George Williams in Context: A Portrait of the Founder of the YMCA*, Sheffield Academic Press.

Boud, D., Keogh, R. and Walker, D. (Eds.) (1985) *Reflection: Turning Experience Into Learning*. Kogan Page.

Bullough, R.V. Jr., Knowles, J.G. and Crow, N.A. (1991) *Emerging as a Teacher*. Routledge.

Cherniss, C. and Egnatios, E. (1978) Clinical Supervision in Community Mental Health. *Social Work*, 23: 3, 219–23.

Christian, C. and Kitto, J. (1987) *The Theory and Practice of Supervision*. YMCA George Williams College.

Dewey, J. (1925) 'Experience and nature'. In Boydson, J.A. (Ed.) (1981) *John Dewey, The Later Works, 1925–1953*, Vol. 1: 1925. Southern Illinois University Press.

Dewey, J. (1933) *How We Think*. D.C. Heath and Co.

Deming, A.L. (1980) Self-actualisation Level as a Predictor of Practicum Supervision Effectiveness. *Journal of Counselling Psychology*, 27: 2, 213–6.

Entwistle, N. (1977) Strategies of Learning and Studying: Recent Research Findings. *British Journal of Educational Studies*, 25, Oct.

Fransson, A. (1977) On Qualitative Differences in Learning IV – Effects of Motivation and Anxiety on Process and Outcome. *British Journal of Educational Psychology*, 47: 3.

Freire, P. (1996) *Pedagogy of the Oppressed*. Rev. edn. Penguin.

Gardiner, D. (1989) *The Anatomy of Supervision: Developing Learning and Professional Competence For Social Work Students*. SRHE 85 Open University Press.

Goffman, E. (1959) *The Presentation of Self in Everyday Life*. Anchor Books.

Green, I. (2009) *A Report Outlining the Conclusions of the Movement Conversation Process*. YMCA England.

Hansen, J.C., Pound, R. and Petro, C. (1976) Review of Research on Practicum Supervision. *Counselor Education and Supervision*, Dec. 107–15.

Henry, W.E., Sims, J.H. and Spray S.L. (1971) *Public and Private Lives of Pschotherapists*. Jossey.

Heppner, P.P. and Handley, P.G. (1981) A Study of the Interpersonal Influence Process in Supervision. *Journal of Counselling and Psychology*, 28: 5, 437–44.

Hess, A.K. (1987) Psychotherapy Supervision: Stages, Buber, and a Theory of Relationship. *Professional Psychology: Research and Practice*, 18: 3, 251–9.

Holloway, E.I. (1982) Interactional Structure of the Supervision Interview. *Journal of Counselling and Psychology*, 29: 3, 309–17.

Hudson, L. (1966) *Contrary Imaginations*. Methuen.

Hutton, J., Quine, C. and Reed, B. (1975) *The Wholeness of Life: The Spiritual Dimension of the YMCA's Work Among Young People*. The National Council of YMCAs.

Itzhaky, H. and Hertzanu-Laty, M. (1999) Application of Martin Buber's Dialogue Theory in Social Work Supervision. *The Clinical Supervisor*, 18: 1, 17–35.

Kadushin, A. (1968) Games People Play in Supervision. *Social Work*, July.

Kadushin, A. (1976) *Supervision in Social Work*, Columbia University Press.

Kadushin, A. (1974) Supervisor-supervisee: A Survey. *Social Work*, 19: 288–97.

Kadushin, A. and Harkness, D. (2002) *Supervision in Social Work*. 4th edn, Columbia University Press.

Karr, J.T. and Geist, G.O. (1977) Facilitation in Supervision as Related to Facilitation in Therapy. *Counselor Education and Supervision*, 16: 4, 263–8.

Kitto, J. (1993) The Nature of Supervision. In *Developing Professional Practice*. (1998) CFS301 Unit 1:3, 1–16, YMCA George Williams College.

Koehler, D. and Harvey, N. (Eds.) (2007) *Blackwell Handbook of Judgment and Decision Making*. Blackwell Publishing.

Kolb, D.A. (1982) *Experiential Learning*. Prentice Hall.

Lanning, W.L.A. (1971) A study of the Relation Between Group and Individual Counselling Supervision and Three Relationship Measures. *Journal of Counselling Psychology*, 18: 5, 401–6.

Laurillard, D. (1978) *The Influence of Context and Cognitive Style on Learning*. University of Surrey: PhD thesis.

McMahon, M. (2003) Supervision and Career Counsellors: A Little-Explored Practice with an Uncertain Future, *British Journal of Guidance and Counselling*, 31: 2, 177–87.

Marton, F. and Saljo, R. (1976) On Qualitative Differences in Learning: Outcome and Process. *British Journal of Educational Psychology*, 46, 4–11.

Maslow, A.H. (1968) *Toward a Psychology of Being*. Van Nostrand.

Milner, R. and Seaman, L. (2008) *YMCA Insync Standards: Core Standards*. YMCA England.

Mistry, T. and Brown, A. (Eds.) (1997) *Race and Groupwork*. Whiting and Birch.

Munro, E. (2011) *The Munro Review of Child Protection Interim Report: The Child's Journey*. Department of Education.

Myles, D. (1998) *YMCAs Working Together*. Tetrahedron Press.

Noble, C. and Irwin, J. (2009) Social Work Supervision: An Exploration of the Current Challenges in a Rapidly Changing Social, Economic and Political Environment. *Journal of Social Work*, 9: 3, 345–58.

O'Hara, M. (1989) Person-centred approach as Conscientizacco: The works of Karl Rogers and Paulo Freire, *Journal of Humanistic Psychology*, 29: 1, 11–36.

Olmstead, J.A. and Christensen, H.E. (1973) *Effects of Agency Work Contexts: An Intensive Field Study*. Department of Health, Education and Welfare.

Pask, G. (1976) Styles and Strategies of Learning. *British Journal of Educational Psychology*, 46: 2, 130–2.

Payne, P.A., Winter, D.E. and Bell, G.E. (1972) Effects of Supervisor Style on The Learning of Empathy in a Supervision Analogue. *Counselor Education and Supervision*, 11: 4, 262–9.

Perry, W.G. (1970) *Forms of Intellectual and Ethical Development in the College Years: A Scheme*. Holt, Rinehart and Winston.

Pierce, R.M. and Schauble, P.G. (1970) Graduate Training of Facilitative Counsellors: The Effects of Individual Supervision. *Journal of Counselling Psychology*, 17: 3, 210–15.

Pritchard, J. (Ed.) (1997) *Good Practice in Supervision in Statutory and Voluntary Organisations*. Jessica Kingsley.

Reid, H.L. (2007) The Shaping of Discourse Positions in the Development of Support and Supervision for Personal Advisers in England. *British Journal of Guidance and Counselling*, 35: 1, 59–77.

Revans, R.W. (1980) *Action Learning*. Biond and Briggs.

Rogers, C.A. (1983) *Freedom to Learn for the 80s*. Charles C. Merrill.

Rosenblatt, A. and Mayer, J.E. (1975) Objectionable Supervisory Styles: Students' Views. *Social Work*, 20: 1984–9.

Saltzberger-Wittenberg, I., Henry, G. and Osborne, E. (1983) *The Emotional Experience of Learning and Teaching*. RKP.

Schon, D.A. (1983) *The Reflective Practitioner: How Professionals Think in Action.* Basic Books.

Social Work Task Force (2009) *Building a Safe and Confident Future* (available online at: http://www.education.gov.uk/publications/eOrderingDownload/01114_2009DOM_EN.pdf

Smith, M.K. (2005) The Functions of Supervision. *Encyclopaedia of Informal Education*, updated 2009.

Stanners, C. (1995) Supervision in the Voluntary Sector. In Pritchard, J. (Ed.) *Good Practice in Supervision: Statutory and Voluntary Organisations.* Jessica Kingsley.

Tash, M.J. (1967) *Supervision in Youth Work: the Report of a 2 Year Training Project in Which Selected Youth Workers Acquired Skills In Supervising.* London Council for Social Service.

Turner, B. (2000) Supervision and Mentoring in Child and Family Social Work: the Role of the First-line Manager in the Implementation of the Post-Qualifying Framework. *Social Work Education*, 19: 3, 231–40.

Yarrow, A. and Millwater, J. (1997) Evaluating the Effectiveness of a Professional Development Course in Supervision and Mentoring. *British Journal of In-service Education*, 23: 3, 349–61.

Witkin, H.A., Moore, C.A. and Goodenough, D.R. (1977) Field-dependent and Field-Independent Cognitive Styles and Their Educational Implications. *Review of Educational Research*, 47, 1–64.

World Alliance of YMCAs – http://www.ymca.int/8.0.html

2

Exploring Coaching and The Role of Supervision

Tina Salter

Introduction

This chapter aims to show the relevance of supervision to the rapidly developing field of coaching, and in the process reinforces the case for a new paradigm of supervision in other areas, including youth work and social work. It has been written in contexts of initial resistance by coaches to being supervised, and of coaches becoming increasingly involved in both youth work and social work, for example in delivering life skills coaching in gaps left by the retreat of service provision due to cuts in funding.

The aim of this chapter is to look at the relationship between supervision and other forms of interaction facilitating reflective practice. The work will provide a critical view of the nature of reflective practice and the various disciplines it might be understood to encompass. In particular it will look at some of the current thinking around the supervision of coaches, and how coaches and organisations see this progressing in the future. Coaching is a fast growing practice worldwide that is, for some, becoming regarded as a form of 'para-supervision'. It is beginning to be deployed in youth work and related areas and might have a role in connection with the aims of social work, in terms of supporting clients into work or in the development of personal and social skills. However, it is helpful for anyone involved in supervision to look at how the focused interaction that coaching is can be supported and perhaps made more effective by supervision, as it provides a strong indication of what supervision is and how it might be carried out.

This being the case, what follows focuses on the relevance or otherwise of supervision in the realm of coaching. The chapter will look at the connections between supervision, coaching and psychotherapy. Overall it examines how supervision might be deployed in coaching contexts, exposes its validity (or otherwise) to other services such as youth and social work, counselling, mentoring and so on.

Figure 2.1 below, provides a straightforward picture of the relative locations of the 'talking encounters' that will be broached and mentioned in this chapter. It is provided as a kind of map that you might want to think about as you read. The positioning of each discipline is to some extent debatable (according to how and why they are deployed) you might be able to see that while they occupy a shared space they are distinctive realms of thought and practice. However, counselling, being, in the main, delivered in a therapeutic sphere, is more closely related to psychotherapy than

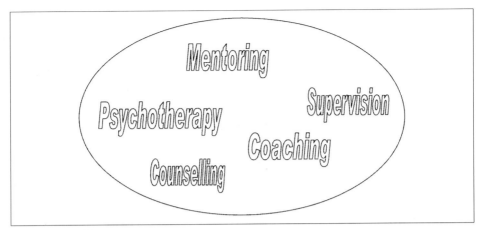

Figure 2.1   Talking encounters

supervision. Supervision is, to a large extent, concerned with the pragmatics of performance enhancement and service delivery in people related arenas. As such it should not essentially be focused on therapeutic concerns, although it may, in some circumstances, have a restorative purpose or outcome.

Coaching

Coaching is a relatively young profession, which embraces:

- an array of people from different backgrounds
- a range of approaches
- a variety of experiences and training

Within this expanse, there is a percentage of practitioners who would describe themselves as coaches, but have not undergone any kind of training or experience of supervision. Whilst there is some quality and influential work going on, the breadth of people naming themselves as coaches worryingly leaves the door wide open to some who do not have any formal qualifications or substantial training.

At the same time, there are indications that some coaches have deliberately avoided any form of coaching training altogether. This could happen for a variety of reasons; but some may feel that their previous academic experiences have provided them with enough knowledge. Whilst not in support of the idea that coaches do not need to undergo training, Bachkirova and Cox highlight a rationale which some adhere to:

There is an argument that exactly because of its practical focus, coaching does not need theories.

Bachkirova and Cox, 2004: 5

However, most of the coaching training organisations or professional membership bodies either insist upon, or highly recommend supervision to varying degrees. This said, there is no single governing body for the coaching profession. So messages are mixed, and not all coaches would want to join a professional body, or necessarily make a choice to take supervision.

Some coaches feel so passionately about supervision that they have formed various groups or associations to share information and look at ways of developing coaching supervision. For example, The Association for Professional Executive Coaches and Supervisors (APECS – see http://www.apecs.org/) not only acts as a membership body, but also provides accredited training for those wanting to develop themselves in this way. It would appear that there is also a strong contingent of coaches who would advocate the need for supervision, seeking to encourage and promote it, as well as ensure that there are enough suitable supervisors to go around.

Some coaches and trainers believe that coaching is closely related to psychology:

> *Psychologists have increasingly and more publicly become involved in the coaching industry. The entry into the coaching arena by psychology, with its attendant rigorous educational programmes and professional ethos and qualifications has, I believe, noticeably raised the bar for the coaching industry in general.*
>
> Grant, 2006: 15

The practice is also seen by some of its practitioners to have a relationship to psychotherapy, so because psychotherapists usually have ongoing clinical supervision post training this acts to endorse the argument that coaches should also continue to take supervision, although it could be validly argued that psychotherapy might warrant different kinds of supportive interventions.

However, without supervision questions inevitably arise about regulating the profession for the benefit of both coaches and clients. If coaches do not receive supervision does this negatively affect their capacity and effectiveness? The obvious answer to this question might be a clear-cut 'yes'; supported practice seems obviously superior to unsupported delivery. But, routinely, the necessary connection between coaching and undertaking supervision to support delivery is not as straightforward as simple logic might suggest.

A wider view

Looking at the potential for, and use of, supervision in coaching can be informative in relation to other professional services.

The term supervision has been interpreted in a variety of ways. Often those coming into a profession will translate the practice according to their previous experience or understanding of it, and these could differ considerably from the kind of approaches and level of support that the coaching membership bodies are working towards. It is therefore important to establish a general understanding of what supervision is and how this might work within the coaching context.

Supervision can be defined largely by each individual's experiences of it – and as the term is used in a range of contexts from retail and selling to counselling and social work, the approach could either be viewed as predominantly managerial or non-managerial. For the purposes of analysis, an understanding of supervision will concentrate on a non-managerial approach (not delivered by a line-manager as supervisor) as this is a more realistic reflection of the kind of supervision taking place within the world of coaching; but it would be worth bearing in mind that those coming into coaching come to it from a wide range of backgrounds, and this can directly affect their desire to be, or not to be supervised in the first instance, and their understanding of the practice.

Frameworks for supervision

APECS is, in many ways, the most prominent coaching supervision body within the profession. They define supervision as:

> *The relationship between the coach and a qualified person who is not in any managerial relationship with the coach wherein the coaching work with particular clients may be discussed in strict confidence with the purpose of enhancing the quality of the coaching work and of ensuring client safety.*
>
> www.apecs.org/pages/ethical-guidelines.php

This sets a context for the kind of ideal that many coaching bodies are looking to work towards. However, Kadushin (1976: 21) explores what supervision means in relation to the field of social work; however his principles have been widely used in related fields including youth and community work. He names 'The principal cluster of functions discharged by the supervisor – administrative, educational and supportive'. The supportive element was something he developed, following Towle (1945: 95) and Burns (1958: 6) who had both defined social work supervision as 'An administrative process with an educational purpose'.

Kadushin suggests that the administrative aspect commissions a level of authority to the supervisor on behalf of the employer who would want to be reassured that the supervisee's work is being carried out professionally, and in an appropriate and strategic way. Even when the supervisor is non-managerial, and not employed by the organisation other than to supervise, they would still have a sense of duty in safe-guarding their profession and acting as a gate-keeper within the parameters of their role.

The educational function of supervision serves to help translate more general learning opportunities either within the organisation (such as training events) or through experiences as a result of their role in a more specific and applied way. Kadushin's development of integrating the supportive function acknowledges the need for interventions by the supervisor which 'Reinforce ego defences and strengthen the capacity of the ego to deal with job stresses and tensions' (Kadushin, 1976: 201).

Bluckert (2006) refers to Kadushin's main supervision functions and suggests that these should be adopted by coaching supervisors.

Christian and Kitto (1987: 2) define supervision as a relationship between supervisor and supervisee in which:

> *The supervisor's job is not to advise or instruct, but to enable the worker (supervisee) to think better about his or her work and, therefore, to work better.*

This definition is not dissimilar to phrases used when defining coaching. It therefore seems highly appropriate that those looking to support others in this way should be agreeable to the view that they also need to buy into the process for themselves.

Rogers (2004) makes the distinction between coaches being coached – where sessions could be shaped by any issue, and being supervised – which would restrict the agenda to professional issues. This is an important part of the debate when looking at some of the varying frameworks used for supervision. Within psychotherapy, counsellors would be expected to undergo therapy themselves as part of their professional training. If this were true of coaching, then coaches would be expected to be coached as well as supervised. However, the two functions are very different. But as Rogers (2004) suggests some forms of supervision draw on principles used within coaching: more likely it is the other way round.

Hawkins and Shohet (2006) argue that supervision should never become too restricted or confined to a uniform approach. They argue for flexibility and outline the importance of prospective supervisors examining the variety of: 'types, aspects and styles that are possible' (2006: 56) in order to carve out their own particular approach to the process.

In discussing the history of supervision, and where the need originally arose from, Christian and Kitto (1987: 1) outline its emergence from the psychoanalytical movement. They discuss the professional deliberations at the time over the need to train and support psychotherapists who worked in difficult and isolating circumstances. However, whilst coaches also work in isolation, the notion of 'difficult circumstances' is perhaps more debatable. Where a psychotherapist would expect to be confronted with a client who was faced with difficult circumstances, this might not always be the case within coaching.

The Association for Coaching (AC) carried out some research in 2005, which led to the production of an organisational policy which provides a rationale for the promotion of supervision. The AC defines coach mentoring/supervision as:

> *A formal and protected time for facilitating in depth reflection for coaches to discuss their work with someone who is experienced in coaching.*
>
> www.associationforcoaching.com/about/ACSuper.doc

However, they fail to make it clear that supervision can be used as a form of quality assurance. Perhaps the best incarnations of both the coaching and supervisory relationship are as collaborative and professional pursuits.

When promoting the discipline, the AC highlights the main benefits of the practice which include: accountability, development and ethical standards. Members are left with the responsibility of selecting their own supervisor and format and context for supervision; however, the AC stipulates that the supervisor must be qualified and a member of a professional coaching body.[6]

At the time of writing, the European Mentoring and Coaching Council (EMCC) have produced an interim statement on supervision, while further work is being carried out to produce a more comprehensive list of guidelines and requirements for members. The statement makes it clear that all members need to have regular supervision and a rationale is given for this. However, the EMCC do acknowledge that the level of supervision will be dependent on the kind of coaching taking place as well as taking into consideration the individual needs of the coach.

It would seem that the majority of coaching bodies are promoting the idea that members should take up supervision as a matter of choice according to personal need and/or context. This may be a reflection of the growing need to find experienced and/or accredited supervisors within an emerging field; so the measure to place choice ahead of obligation may perhaps be more a sign of problems in terms of supply and demand than any hard and fast ethical or practical attachment to preference. However the commitment to choice presents some problems which are not mentioned. When choosing a supervisor already known to the supervisee, they may select someone who has a similar world view to their own. This could affect the learning potential available within the supervisory situation compared with a supervisee matched with someone with different experiences, background and outlook. However, if a supervisor comes from a completely different cultural or organisational context relative to the supervisee, this risks heightening the chances of misunderstanding, confusion and even clashes in terms of delivery approaches and standards.

Rogers (2004) points out the possibility of both coach and supervisor sharing the same blind spots, which could encourage important aspects to be missed. She concludes by saying that supervision needs to be set up in a way which meets the needs of the individual coach: the way in which it is done, at what level and the frequency of sessions. At first reading this feels reasonable, but it creates a potentially chaotic macro-situation, wherein any ambition to develop generally fair, transparent, consistent and disciplined practice across the discipline is replaced by a very loose, laisser faire response, hardly amenable to determining overall effectiveness, comprehension, regulation or coherent, appropriate safeguarding.

For all this, on the whole, it appears that coaching bodies are in agreement that supervision is to be welcomed and encouraged. However, the degree to which they become involved in the selection and monitoring process of supervisors varies; the majority would not currently impose supervision on their members.

---

[6]For a compact outline of the nature and practice of mentoring see http://www.cipd.co.uk/subjects/lrnanddev/coachmntor/mentor.htm

Regulation

One of the organisational objectives of the AC is to:

> *Promote and support development of accountability and credibility across the industry and supervision is part of this strategy.*
>
> www.associationforcoaching.com/memb/ACSuper2.doc

On the AC website there is also a statement which explains how supervision is valued and put into practice for current members:

> *We regard supervision that focuses on client progress and coach/client relationships as a key element in facilitating learning and ensuring quality control of coaching activity.*
>
> www.associationforcoaching.com

It is interesting to note here that the issue of regulation is insinuated as an important feature of supervision, alongside exploration of practice. In terms of how that works out in practice, this is not undertaken on a one-to-one basis:

> *Case discussion facilitated by an experienced supervisor will take place in groups to maximise the opportunity for learning from each other's experiences.*
>
> www.academyofexecutivecoaching.com/display.asp?type=6andmenu=411andid=393

While this approach may be more effective resource-wise, it does not always produce the best results for the individual. For instance, when participating as part of a group, some may feel more inhibited to make contributions compared with when they are alone with a supervisor. This, of course, can operate the other way round; some people being more likely to contribute in groups than in one-to-one situations, but competitiveness can also feature as part of group dynamics, which can prove to be a distorting feature in terms of the accuracy of response. Whilst there are benefits to group supervision, such as a greater variety of shared experiences and views, as the only suggested format for receiving supervision this approach is inherently limiting.

APECS outline the requirements for supervision of their membership. These include making appropriate choices of a supervisor which best fits their learning needs, and discussing their thoughts, feelings and reactions to their work. Supervisors registered with APECS are required to provide an annual report on their supervisees, which helps to assure the organisation that they are working ethically and to an acceptable standard. APECS also offer the option of becoming an Accredited Supervisor of Executive Coaches.

Whilst APECS have developed a clear strategy for coaching supervision, this is limited to the Executive models of coaching and would therefore exclude other types of coaching.

Bluckert's view (2006) is based on his previous supervision experiences as a social worker and counsellor before moving into the realms of coaching. For him supervision is one of the main regulating methods, particularly as the profession is still emerging.

It would appear that part of a membership body's role is to regulate members, and supervision can be (and usually is) used as a means to check that coaches are operating to and complying with organisational frameworks of good practice. However, the range of professional bodies have different ways of regulating, and therefore this leaves the coach who is a member of one organisation the option of going elsewhere if they are challenged or unwilling to conform. In addition to this there are the coaches who have no perceived need to belong to a professional body. Coaches are not dependent on having a membership status which enables them to access clients; as such any current attempts to regulate would be confined to individual membership organisations.

Quality

Arney (2006) comments on the research concluding that supervision is a given for the coaching profession, and coaches need to accept that this should be a regular feature of their working role. However whilst the majority of the coaching bodies have vocalised their support of coaching supervision, and some have consulted their members, it could be argued that those who hold opposing views may not have had any opportunities to communicate their views if they have not taken out membership.

Clutterbuck and Megginson (1999) argue the case for a good supervisor facilitating a safe place to discuss issues, allowing for creative energy to work on fresh ideas and solutions.

Carroll (2006) explores the value of supervision for coaching psychologists and organisations that make use of their services. One of the main themes highlighted was experiential learning having a greater effect than being taught, and how supervision can make use of reflective practice to ensure that learning takes place. This relies on the supervisor having a comprehensive understanding of the supervisee's learning style in order to effectively facilitate this process. While this seems like a very high ambition for any relationship (guaranteed learning, complete consciousness of another's learning style, given that the person concerned can be categorised as responding significantly more to one style than others) this echoes the point which Kadushin makes about supervision having an educative role.

Carroll (2006) touches on a lack of information and training available for supervisees which could help them feel more prepared for sessions. Rogers (2004) comments on this as well and includes tips on getting the most out of supervision. Perhaps this is something which could be explored further with coaches.

Butwell (2006: 43) writes in the *International Journal of Evidence Based Coaching and Mentoring* an article based on some research she did with a group supervision forum over the space of a year. She sought to 'Understand whether supervision provides real value to coaches, by observing the experiences of group supervision'. Her findings concluded that the sharing of cases was the most valuable aspect of the process. She identified a need for organisations to develop guidelines for internal supervision mechanisms which help to ensure the quality of professional development and supervision for their coaches.

It seems that the quality of coaching supervision is dependent upon finding a suitable supervisor who has a good understanding of coaching in addition to the skills required of an excellent supervisor. At the same time, a coach needs to be in a position to be able to make use of supervision, so perhaps they need more education on how to get the best out of supervision. But of course this is a chicken and egg situation; the coach who is not keen to undertake supervision is perhaps not in the best place to undertake education on how to get the best from it.

All of these factors do not account for coaches who are not interested in supervision, yet provide a high quality service to their clients. Taking this view into account, this raises the issue of assessment, and the possibility of weighing up the supervisory needs of the coach (if any), based on the quality of service to clients as well as the quality of supervision on offer.

Approaches to supervision within organisations

Whilst coaches often work as freelancers, it is not uncommon for contractual agreements to be made on the basis that coaches are receiving either their own supervision, or from the company employing the coach. This will be seen as a way of selecting services where accountability has been built in and also used as a safe-guard for those entrusting them with a potentially influential role in terms of individual and general practice.

Supervision can also be contracted in by similar arrangement. Clutterbuck and Megginson (1999) refer to a case study of a coaching and counselling practice that employed an external supervisor to develop the team through group and individual sessions. They liken this role to that of a mentor, and this could have been due to the style which is described as 'one of persistent questioning interspersed with advice and suggested approaches' (Clutterbuck and Megginson, 1999: 60). This has a slightly different emphasis to the style described by Rogers (2004) which does not seek to give advice. Interestingly, as this form of supervision used both group and individual approaches, there were opportunities to explore team dynamics when working together. They attributed the success of this task to the rapport and relationship of trust which had been built up with the supervisor.

Rogers goes on to unravel some of the complex organisational systems which vary in the degree of external verses internal parties. For instance, an awareness of needs and responsibilities could be limited if an internal coach is being supervised externally.

Research carried out by The Chartered Institute of Personnel and Development (CIPD) published in 2006 was entitled: 'Coaching Supervision – Maximising the Potential of Coaching'. Amongst other findings, the research discovered that a quarter of organisations that use coaches provide them with regular supervision, and 44 per cent of coaches have regular supervision. Arney (2006) raises the issue of confidentiality, given that some coaches are working for organisations that are internally providing them with a supervisor. She suggests that the key factor is discussing at the contracting stage what happens with the information that is disclosed, and where the boundaries lie for the coach in supervision sessions. This is always going to be subjected to legal and organisational requirements of course, but talking these over can raise personal and professional consciousness and be educational in itself.

The way in which supervision is set up will vary according to the nature of work the coach is undertaking. When supervision is stipulated either through a membership body or via work commissioned from a company contracting the coaching, the arrangements will need to be taken into consideration; any possible impacts these could have on the coachee need to be discussed with the relevant parties from the outset.

Other professions which use supervision

Whilst supporting the need for supervision, Rogers (2004) challenges some of the grandiose claims made about its potential impact. For example, she critiques the social work profession in having a supervision system in place for more than 40 years, but child protection scandals have continued to prevail (2004: 173). She also argues that there are many other people-intensive professions which have not historically gone down the supervision road; and she challenges the notion that supervision is a guarantee of the quality of coaching. A validation of this is that there is no definitive evidence that supervision improves practice in any sphere. In fact it is arguable that in many instances, even cross professionally, it exists, sometimes overtly, often more subtly, as a means of quality assurance.

Driscoll has written about the practice of clinical supervision for the healthcare profession, which includes a chapter entitled: 'Exploring the potential of professional coaching for the growth of clinical supervision in practice'. The purpose of this chapter has come about as a result of Driscoll (2007: 137–8) sensing that healthcare professionals have adopted supervision without perhaps fully understanding its potential, and an exploration of coaching could help add value to their supervision system. He suggests that an alliance between the healthcare and coaching professions could be mutually beneficial:

> Perhaps some of the lessons and expertise of developing clinical supervision in UK healthcare over the last decade might offer the emerging profession of coaching a way forward that require practising coaches to also engage in 'regular' supervision as part of their continuing professional development.

This of course would open a huge market to coaching. The coaching industry as it stands today is incredibly diverse. Incorporated into the field are coaches ranging from sports to business to psychology and a whole host of other areas in between. This might to some extent make coaches uneasy about making structures and frameworks too rigid, which might exclude some coaches in areas which did not lend themselves naturally to supervision. At the same time many task-orientated coaches feel that they do not require supervision. In some cases though, it might be difficult to know where to draw the line. Which aspects of coaching are purely task or skill-orientated, and which only address issues of a more internal nature? Surely there are many contexts where one side drifts into the other, and vice versa.

As coaches are not currently dependent on having supervision in order to recruit clients, it might prove difficult for any association to come up with definitions which may then exclude some who currently describe themselves as a coach. And if supervision is included as a general standard for all, this also may act as an excluding factor.

Whether the range of contexts a coach works in affects their need for supervision, or the individual coaching style addresses external or internal factors of the coachee, needs to be acknowledged and taken into consideration if supervision becomes a requirement of all coaches.

Conclusion

While supervision might have the potential, when experienced to a high standard, to have a significant benefit on both the coach and those whom they serve, it should also be appreciated that some coaches utilise other kinds of resources and interventions that help them develop; or the kind of coaching they are delivering does not warrant regular ongoing supervision. But logic suggests that if one is a great believer in coaching, then one, to be consistent, should also want to put oneself through a similar but perhaps more defined process. This, rationally would be focused on exploring with someone else one's own ways of developing and moving forward as a coach. Why would a practitioner be opposed to supervision when they are themselves dependent on others wanting to set goals with them as a coach?

The EMCC has concluded at the time of writing that the industry is not ready for supervision to be enforced. This begs the question when it will be ready, if ever? But that does not take away the need to promote and make supervision available to those at least starting out in coaching.

Referring back to the historical aspect, and the original circumstances in which supervision was introduced into the psychoanalytical movement, it was about an identified gap needing to be filled: providing more training and support for those facing difficult professional situations. It is probably not the case that the vast majority of coaches are crying out for more training and support due to the many difficult client circumstances they are facing. However many coaches do recognise a need for supervision, if only for the maintenance of standards, and they can also identify with the issue of working in isolation, as such being able to value appropriate support and guidance.

References

Arney, E. (2006) Insider's Guide. *People Management*, 23 November.

Association for Coaching (2005) *Supervision Report.* Association for Coaching.

Bachkirova, T. and Cox, E. (2004) A Bridge Over Troubled Water, Bringing Together Coaching and Counselling. *The International Journal of Mentoring and Coaching*, II, 1.

Beinart, H. (2004) Models of Supervision and The Supervisory Relationship and Their Evidence Base. In Fleming, I. and Steen, L. (Eds.) *Supervision and Clinical Psychology: Theory, Practice and Perspectives.* Brunner-Routledge.

Bluckert, P. (2006) *Psychological Dimensions to Executive Coaching.* Open University Press.

Bryant Jefferies, R. (2005) *Person-Centred Counselling Supervision: Personal and professional.* Radcliffe.

Burns, M.E. (1958) *Historical Development of the Process of Casework Supervision.* University of Chicago.

Butwell, J. (2006) Group Supervision for Coaches: is it Worthwhile? A Study of The Process in a Major Professional Organisation. *International Journal of Evidence Based Coaching and Mentoring*, 4: 2.

Carroll, M. (2006) Key Issues in Coaching Psychology. *The Coaching Psychologist*, 2: 1.

Chartered Institute of Personnel and Development (2006) *Coaching Supervision.* A paper prepared for the CIPD coaching conference.

Christian, C. and Kitto, J. (1987) *The Theory and Practice of Supervision.* Occasional paper 1, The Centre for Professional Studies in Informal Education.

Clutterbuck, D. and Megginson, D. (1999) *Mentoring Executives and Directors.* Elsevier Butterworth Heinemann.

DCP (2003) *Discussion paper: DCP policy on continued supervision.* British Psychological Society.

Driscoll, J. (2007) *Practising Clinical Supervision: A Reflective Approach For Healthcare Professionals.* Elsevier Limited.

Dryden, W. and Thorne, B. (1991). *Training and Supervision for Counselling in Action.* Sage.

European Mentoring and Coaching Council (2004) *Code of Ethics.* EMCC.

European Mentoring and Coaching Council (2004) *Guidelines on Supervision: An Interim Statement.* EMCC.

Feltham, C. and Dryden, W. (1994) *Developing Counsellor Supervision.* Sage.

Grant, A. (2006) A Personal Perspective on Coaching and the Development of Coaching Psychology. *International Coaching Psychology Review*, 1: 1.

Hawkins, P. and Shohet, R. (2006) *Supervision in the Helping Professions.* 3rd edn, Open University Press.

Kadushin, A. (1976) *Supervision in Social Work.* Columbia University Press.

Laireiter, A-R. and Willutzki, U. (2003) Self-reflection and Self-Practice in Training of Cognitive Behaviour Therapy: An Overview. *Clinical Psychology and Psychotherapy*, 10, 19–30.

Leonard, T.J. (1999) *Becoming a Coach: The Coach U Approach.* Coach U Press.

Marken, M. and Payne, M. (1987) *Enabling and Ensuring: Supervision in Practice.* National Youth Bureau.

Myler, S. (2007) *Supervision for Therapists: A Critique.* www.ezinearticles.com (accessed 24 May)

Page, S. and Wosket, V. (1994) *Supervising the Counsellor: A clinical model.* Routledge.

Proctor, B. (2000) *Group Supervision: A guide to Creative Space.* Sage.

Rogers, J. (2004) *Coaching Skills.* Open University Press.

Rose, M.L. and Best, D.L. (2005) *Transforming Practice through Clinical Education, Professional Supervision and Mentoring.* Churchill Livingstone.

Shipton, G. (1997) *Supervision of Psychotherapy and Counselling: Making a Place to Think.* Open University Press.

Smith, M. (1996) *The Functions of Supervision.* YMCA George Williams College.

Tight, M., Morton-Cooper, A. and Palmer, A. (1993) *Mentoring, Preceptorship and Clinical Supervision: A Guide to Clinical Support and Supervision.* Blackwell Publishing.

Towle, C. (1945) *Common Human Needs.* US Dept. of Health, Education and Welfare.

Useful web references

http://www.academyofexecutivecoaching.com/display.asp?type =6andmenu=411andid=393

http://www.apecs.org/pages/ethical-guidelines.php

http://www.apecs.org/pages/criteria-guidelines.php

http://www.associationforcoaching.com/about/ACSuper.doc
http://www.coachingsupervisionacademy.com/full_spectrum_model.phtml
http://www.emccouncil.org/downloads/EMCC_Guidelines_On_Supervision.PDF
http://www.pbcoaching.com/article-coaching-supervision.php

3

Dialogue and Dialectic

Justin Hill and Brian Belton

Whatever the limitations of particular types of practice it is broadly agreed in the literature that supervision which includes the development of knowledge and under-standing via reviewing practice, questioning theory, implicating research, consideration and critical reflection, is likely to give rise to wisdom, insight and awareness. This exemplifies the best fruits of education. As such the ethos of supervision, in its best incarnation, is educational, but the fabric of supervision is dialogue.

If you think about it, that seems a fairly obvious statement; the warp and weft of the encounter, like psychotherapy and counselling, is conversational, a stream of orated ideas, statements, questions and impressions. But this, on the face of it, is no different to chats, gossiping, chin wagging, chewing the fat, maybe debate or the confessional; youth work is said to be founded on dialogue (see Jeffs and Smith, 1987 for example). While these forms of interaction are often part of, or even at times take over or subvert supervision, dialogue, in the supervision context, needs more explanation. For Hill (2005: 16)

> *Engaging in critical reflection with students has been one of the most rewarding experiences of my professional career. I have found that if I start by having faith in our ability to engage in dialogue; demonstrate my humility regarding the incom-pleteness of my knowledge; and show my commitment and enthusiasm, a relationship of mutual trust is established.*

'Trust' is a recurring concept in writing and debate about supervision/reflective practice. It is widely agreed that once a relationship of trust develops sufficiently, supervisees are more able to question considerations, such as the influence of the supervisor, the agency's value base, particular constraints of the practice setting, the authority of the university to set course requirements and assess work or even the value base of youth work itself. Thus confusion and directionless is replaced by the motivation towards a renewed sense of commitment and engagement.

The trust that facilitates this metamorphosis develops by way and out of dialogue, which at best, transforms into a dialectical exchange/relationship. This might be understood as a similar process consistently described by Freire. It is also intrinsic in the educational philosophy of Martin Buber.

However, Buber would argue that dialectic is at the heart of dialogue. This seems to put the situation the other way round, but in practice movement from dialogue to dialectic is not a finished journey. For Buber, it is via dialogue that what might start out as apparently contrary positions (or truths) can be maintained and accommodated in dialectic. This is quite different to mere displacement or replacement of ideas.

It may appear that this chapter strays from this perspective, in that dialectic is presented as the interplay of existing ideas being discussed and new understandings developing, rather than what Buber would see as its consequence; a 'unity of contraries'. So straightforwardly, it would be understandable if the reader took it that dialectic is merely a stage on from dialogue. However, the move into dialectic, beyond dialogue, necessarily leads to a return to dialogue, because, as Buber insisted, all ideas must not be held fast but brought back to the encounter of dialogue. If this were not the case dialectic would end with a sort of 'master idea', which is a contradiction to any commitment to dialectical discourse or an educational/enlightening process.

However, the maintaining or accommodation of 'truths', even holding contradictory notions together by way of a sort of creative tension, leaves us risking, as Foucault (1972) might have it, turning documents into monuments; whilst an idea might be a synthesis of two or more ideas, it is, nonetheless, a new idea in itself. So in the following model, the shifting from dialogue to dialectic to dialogue is neither positing a displacement nor a conservationist notion in terms of ideas or truths. It might be better understood as a conception based on development and growth of perspective, awareness and understanding.

Many agencies in the youth work sphere, perhaps relying primarily on volunteers, have some structure in place for the provision of work supervision.[7] This commitment is premised on the belief that supervision will result in the development of practitioner skill and knowledge and so enhance agency product and delivery (for example Kadushkin and Harkness, 2002).

Buber's concept of dialogue is the foundation of his philosophy of education. For him, dialogue is real living, direct knowing and a glimpse of the absolute. Buber argues that, experiencing the world is insufficient to becoming fully human; one must stand in relation to the world through dialogue. Furthermore, the true nature of knowledge is dialogical, because it cannot be separated from the knowing subject. Buber does not seek to set out a proof for his vision of dialogue: he offers his insight as a challenge and testimony, more than a justification.

Although one cannot generate dialogue directly through effort, there are both preconditions for dialogue and factors which inhibit its occurrence. Preconditions include grace, defined as 'the spontaneously undetermined presence of mutuality' (Kramer, 2003: 22). Dialogue requires that the partners in the supervision encounter be openly attentive, fully present, genuine and sincere, demonstrating respect (see Kramer, 2003).

When, instead of responding to others as unique persons, we treat them as objects among objects, as projected images that fit the structure of our knowledge, we disrupt our capacity to encounter them as totally exceptional beings, with their own essence

---

[7]According to Munro (2011a) 'Volunteers working with children and families require regular and skilled supervision' (5.2: 75).

and presence; as whole and extraordinary entities (Kramer, 2003: 20; 46). This level of interaction facilitates education, awareness, enlightenment, revelation and, at times forms of epiphany. In short it is argued that through dialogical encounter human living can be fulfilled.

Education based on dialogue can be understood as an alternative to traditional education practice, which has been characterised as a process whereby experts transmit information for learners to passively receive:

> *There is a new awareness now, that on all the major problems that face the modern world, no experts have all the answers. Each may have valuable information to contribute, but we need dialogue to draw in the insights of all who are concerned as we search for solutions.*
>
> Hope and Timmel, 1996: 17

Freire (1972: 75) devotes a chapter to elucidating his concept of dialogue in education. For Freire, this always involves both action and reflection 'Thus, to speak a true word is to transform the world'. For Freire, dialogue humanises, and education without dialogue can only objectify, oppress and indoctrinate:

> *Without dialogue there is no communication, and without communication there can be no true education.*
>
> Freire, 1972: 81

Participants in dialogue should learn from each other, not simply impose their views and debate from fixed positions:

> *. . . dialogue cannot be reduced to the act of one person's 'depositing' ideas in another, nor can it be a simple exchange of ideas to be 'consumed' by the discussants. Nor yet is it a hostile, polemical argument between men who are committed neither to the naming of the world, nor to the search for truth, but rather to the imposition of their own truth.*
>
> Ibid: 77

Vella (2002: 3; 10) notes that the literal, etymological meaning of dialogue is 'the word between us' or 'through relationship'. Freire suggests that the term dialogue '. . . is not simply another word for a mere conversation among people about everyday matters' Freire, in Leistyna, 1999: 46.

However, for Smith (2001: 7):

> *We should . . . not make too much of the differences between conversation and dialogue. In common sense terms dialogue could be seen as a form of conversation – a particular 'serious' format.*

Whilst everyday conversations may seem insignificant in comparison to critical dialogue, Smith (2001: 7) suggests that informal educators (here he is chiefly referring to youth workers) make more regular use of conversation than dialogue, and that 'seemingly trivial exchanges' can actually be very important in terms of being and belonging. Arnett (1992: 4) agrees, suggesting that rather than necessarily concerning 'special moments of great depth of conversation', dialogue in education is founded on ideas, relationships and values.

Dialogue has been contrasted with debate, as an alternative form of public discourse that avoids characterising issues as a battle between two opposing sides (Tannen, 1998). However, Freire's conception of dialogue cannot be reduced to a method to be chosen from a repertoire – it is a process of finding meaning together, and a way of apprehending the world:

> *I think that in an attempt to understand the meaning of the dialogical process we have to put aside any possibility of understanding it as pure tactics or strategy . . . dialogue . . . is a way of knowing and not a tactic to involve.*

Freire, in Leistyna, 1999: 46

Burbules (1993) envisions educational dialogue as a game, with various possible moves and three rules:

- participation
- commitment
- reciprocity

In creating a model of dialogue, with a taxonomy of dialogical genres, Burbules reduces dialogue to strategy and tactics in a way resisted by Freire. Robinson (1995: 249) in contrast, suggests that Burbules has been insufficiently rigorous in pursuing a model of dialogue, stating that:

> . . . *an adequate account of dialogue must be centrally concerned with the psychology, including the motivation, of those who engage in it; with normative questions of dialogical quality and with the practical utility of the proposed model.*

Arnett (1992: 11) argues that dialogue cannot be a formula because each relationship 'offers a different and unique starting place for discourse.' However, he is prepared to acknowledge some foundational conditions for dialogue, including: starting from a position of openness to the possibility of changing one's mind in the light of new evidence; and a commitment to maintaining positive regard towards partners in dialogue. Similarly, Oesterreicher (1986: 99) notes ' . . . dialogue is not surrender; it is rather the arduous task of listening to, and learning from, one another'.

This feels very important in terms of achieving an educational encounter. How can I learn from you if you are not ready, willing and able to learn about me from me? This might be thought of as the defining question that separates mere instruction or orders from the experience of education; to teach others one must be able to learn from them – for the student to learn from the tutor they must be in a place where they are prepared to teach the tutor about them as a starting point. This does not limit the capacity of the student to only teaching about themselves, but provides a foundation for both tutor and student to develop more general and broad insights about the nature of learning and the character of the educational process they are mutually involved in.

Smith (2001: 1) states that the concept of dialogue in education is mostly associated with Freire, Gadamer, Habermas, Bohm and Buber. He notes that:

> Today, when the word 'dialogue' is spoken in educational circles, it is often linked to Paulo Freire. The same is true of 'subject' and 'object'. Yet, in the twentieth century, it is really in the work of Martin Buber that the pedagogical worth of dialogue was realised.

Buber's philosophy of dialogue is at the heart of his approach to education (Friedman, 2002). For Buber, no amount of experiencing the world is sufficient to become fully human: one must encounter the world through dialogue. Like Freire, Buber insists that dialogue is a way of knowing: to enter into dialogue is to gain knowledge directly from being fully present in a unique situation. This knowledge cannot be reduced or crystallised into either subjective opinion or objective fact.

Bingham and Sidorkin (2004) cite Buber as a theoretical source for their pedagogy of relation: this is an umbrella term for educational approaches that recognise the primacy of relations over the isolated self. Thayer-Bacon (2004: 178) for example, discusses John Dewey's terms interaction and transaction, noting that:

> Whereas 'interaction' treated individuals as if they were autonomous, like billiard balls that bounce off each other without changing as a result, 'transaction' emphasises that individuals are not autonomous, but are always in relation with others and are always already affecting each other.

Similarly, Buber insisted that being – in and of itself – is an abstraction from the essential lived reality of being-in-relation (Vogel, 1970). Bingham and Sidorkin (2004) suggest that there is empirical evidence of a practical need for relational educational theory, to counter the prevailing technicist approach that solely concentrates on teaching academic skills and content. Arnett (1992: 6) expresses concern that universities may be providing knowledge whilst failing to 'offer an education beyond questions of self-advancement.' In recommending an approach based on dialogue, he cites John Gardner, who fears that tertiary education can lead to:

> . . . an overvaluing of intellect as against character, of getting there first as against growing in mind and spirit, of food for the ego as against food for the hunger of the heart.
>
> Gardner, cited in Arnett, 1992: 6

In the same way, Buber (2002a: 123) insists that any education 'worthy of the name' is education of character. This does not imply that dialogue in education can be constant, or even sustained over a long period. Buber speaks of fleeting glimpses of dialogue. Arnett (1992: 32) notes that the educational institution that pushes every student to learn dialogically 'will invite a "tyranny of intimacy"'. So, although education cannot

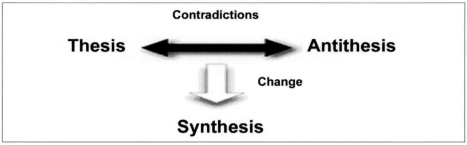

Figure 3.1   Dialectic

solely consist of dialogue, through dialogue education can '... develop students' character in a way that would enable them to live in society humanely' (Morgan 2007: 11).

Dialectic

Much of what is referred to as dialogical interaction is in fact dialectical. The supervisory interaction, for it to be both educational and informative, needs to aim for more than a straightforward dialogical situation. In the best of all possible worlds supervisor and supervisee, if each are to realise being both teacher and learner, need to be aiming to promote 'dialectic'. This, straightforwardly, is a situation wherein ideas can shared and so developed in order to promote new ideas and insights. Figure 3.1 outlines this process:

Here you can see that one (supervisor or supervisee) starts off with an idea (Thesis). This demands to be met with ideas that might challenge or enlarge that idea (Antithesis). This brings about a new understanding (the two perspectives coming together – the Synthesis)

Figure 3.2 illustrates this as a sort of 'intellectual pathway' for developing our understanding of reality:

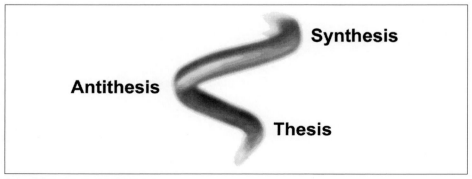

Figure 3.2   Intellectual pathway

As you can see, in education terms this is a leap forward from simplistic dialogue, where knowledge and insight can be 'held fast, preserved or factually transmitted' (Buber, 1976: 69). Moments of dialogue: ... *appear as strange lyrics and dramatic episodes, seductive and magical, but tearing us away to dangerous extremes, loosening the well-tried context, leaving more questions than satisfaction behind them, shattering security* (Buber, 2004: 32). It is all too easy for the supervisor to dominate the process via their aims to educate the supervisee which they are sometimes tasked to effect by employers, even though the supervisee might feel or be told they are making the pace and creating the agenda (the supervisee avoids learning by simply going along with the supervisor – for a quiet life). This dialectical process of mutual discovery might be understood as the sort of interaction one might expect following the establishment of dialogue. It complements dialogue (and dialogue allows it) while providing insights that can be expressed, as opposed to what might be thought of as a 'stationary dialogue', where the insights cannot be expressed or transmitted. However, the above spiral might be thought of as potentially eternal rather than the picture of a whole journey.

For all this, the point is for both parties involved (although more than two people might be implicated) in the dialectic, to share the overt aim to develop insight, understanding and awareness. It is a different process to that premised on the aim that the supervisee should somehow simply learn from or be educated by the supervisor. This would in fact not be education at all; it might be thought of at best to be advice giving, instruction or confessional (perhaps encompassing symbolic or actual absolution and penitence) at worse it could be understood as indoctrination, domination or colonisation.

Somewhat counter to Buber's insistence on relationship, suggesting the involvement of more than one person,[8] dialectic, being a sort of 'ideas factory' does not, of necessity, require more than individual commitment. This is a dialectical experience and a learning process that arises out of a dialogical commitment and it can happen while reading, watching the television, viewing a painting or a landscape – questioning what is and allowing what is to respond to you can transform from a dialogical to dialectical experience. Whereas dialogue always arises between two subjects dialectical reasoning can be internal to one. In relation to supervision this understanding is imperative as it as one of the channels that can provide material for the professional scrutiny that supervision is. Practice of this kind of interaction with the world helps us form our questions about situations and events, that can be taken to supervision as the basis of dialogue with the supervisor, so feeding the potential for professional dialectic. This process is essential to the betterment of professional delivery of services.

References

Arnett, R.C. (1992) *Dialogic Education: Conversation About Ideas and Between Persons*. Southern Illinois University Press.

---

[8]Buber discusses the possibility of dialogue with non-humans and inanimate objects (e.g.: a tree in the first part of *I and Thou*)

Bingham, C. and Sidorkin, A.M. (2004) The Pedagogy of Relation: An Introduction. In Bingham, C. and Sidorkin, A.M. (Eds.) *No Education Without Relation.* Peter Lang.

Buber, M. (1948) *Hasidism.* Philosophical Library.

Buber, M. (1952) *Eclipse of God.* Harper and Row.

Buber, M. (1957) *Pointing the Way.* Routledge and Kegan Paul.

Buber, M. (1964) *Daniel: Dialogues on Realisation.* Holt Rinehart and Winston.

Buber, M. (1967a) *Kingship of God.* George Allen and Unwin.

Buber, M. (1967b) Replies to my Critics. In Schilpp, P.A. and Friedman, M. *The Philosophy of Martin Buber.* Cambridge University Press.

Buber, M. (1970) *I and Thou*, T. & T. Clark (W. Kaufmann translation).

Buber, M. (1972) *On Judaism.* Schocken.

Buber, M. (1988) *The Knowledge of Man.* Humanities Press International.

Buber, M. (1991) *Tales of the Hasidim.* Schocken Books.

Buber, M. (1996) *Ecstatic Confessions: The Heart of Mysticism.* Syracuse University Press.

Buber, M. (1997a) *Good and Evil.* Prentice Hall.

Buber, M. (1997b) *Israel and the World: Essays in a Time of Crisis.* Syracuse University Press.

Buber, M. (2000a) *Hasidism and Modern Man.* Humanity Books.

Buber, M. (2000b) *On the Bible: Eighteen Studies.* Syracuse University Press.

Buber, M. (2002a) *Between Man and Man.* Routledge.

Buber, M. (2002) *The Way of Man.* Routledge.

Buber, M. (2003) *Two Types of Faith.* Syracuse University Press.

Buber, M. (2004) *I and Thou.* 2nd edn, Continuum (R.G. Smith Translation).

Burbules, N.C. (1993) *Dialogue in Teaching: Theory and Practice.* Teachers College Press.

Burgess, H., Sieminski, S. and Arthur, L. (2006) *Achieving Your Doctorate in Education.* Sage.

Cohen, A. (1983) *The Educational Philosophy of Martin Buber.* Associated University Presses.

Foucault, F. (1972) *The Archaeology of Knowledge.* Routledge.

Freire, P. (1972) *Pedagogy of the Oppressed*. Herder and Herder.

Friedman, M. (1964) Interrogation of Martin Buber. In Rome, S. and Rome, B. (Eds.) *Philosophical Interrogations.* Holt, Rinehart and Winston.

Friedman, M. (1965) Martin Buber's Final Legacy: 'The Knowledge of Man'. *Journal for the Scientific Study of Religion*, 5: 1, 4–9.

Friedman, M. (1967) Bibliography. In Schilpp, P.A. and Friedman, M. *The Philosophy of Martin Buber.* Cambridge University Press.

Friedman, M. (1984) Martin Buber's Approach to Comparative Religion. In Gordon, H. and Bloch, J. (Eds.) *Martin Buber: A Centenary Volume.* Ktav Publishing House: Ben-Gurion University of the Negev.

Friedman, M. (1988) *Martin Buber's Life and Work: The Early Years 1878–1923.* Wayne State University Press.

Friedman, M. (1988) *Martin Buber's Life and Work: The Middle Years 1923–1945.* Wayne State University Press.

Friedman, M. (1988) *Martin Buber's Life and Work: The Later Years 1945–1965.* Wayne State University Press.

Friedman, M. (2002a) Introduction. In Buber, M. *Between Man and Man.* Routledge.

Friedman, M. (2002) *Martin Buber: The Life of Dialogue.* 4th edn, Routledge.

Hill, J. (2005) *Select Two Important Theorists in Adult Education and Critically Examine and Compare their Ideas*, unpublished.

Hope, A. and Timmel, S. (1996) *Training for Transformation.* Mambo Press.

Jeffs, T. and Smith, M. (Eds.) (1987) *Youth Work.* Palgrave Macmillan.

Kadushin, A. and Harkness, P. (2002) *Supervision in Social Work.* 4th edn. Columbia University Press.

Kaufmann, W. (1967) Buber's Religious Significance. In Schilpp, P.A. and Friedman, M. *The Philosophy of Martin Buber.* Cambridge University Press.

Kramer, K.P. (2003) *Martin Buber's I and Thou.* Paulist Press.

Leistyna, P. (1999) *Presence of Mind: Education and the Politics of Deception.* Westview.

Morgan, W.J. (2007) Martin Buber: Philosopher of Dialogue and of the Resolution of Conflict. *British Academy Review*, 10: 11–4.

Munro, E. (2011a) *The Munro Review of Child Protection: Final Report. A child-centred System.* Department of Education.

Oesterreicher, J.M. (1986) *The Unfinished Dialogue: Martin Buber and the Christian Way.* Philosophical Library.

Robinson, V.M.J. (1995) Dialogue Needs a Point and a Purpose. *Educational Theory*, 45: 2, 235–49.

Simon, E. (1967) Martin Buber, The Educator. In Schilpp, P.A. and Friedman, M. *The Philosophy of Martin Buber.* Cambridge University Press.

Smith, M.K. (2001) *Dialogue and Conversation, the encyclopaedia of informal education*, www.infed.org/biblio/b-dialog.htm last updated in 2001

Tannen, D. (1998) *The Argument Culture: Moving from Debate to Dialogue.* Random House.

Thayer-Bacon, B.J. (2004) Personal and Social Relations in Education. In Bingham, C. and Sidorkin, A.M. (Eds.) *No Education Without Relation.* Peter Lang.

Vella, J. (2002). *Learning to Listen, Learning to Teach: The Power of Dialogue in Educating Adults.* Jossey-Bass.

4

Buber, Education, Dialogue and Supervision

Justin Hill and Brian Belton

Introduction

This chapter focuses on the educational aims and task of supervision through the lens of Martin Buber's analysis of dialogue. This facilitates a critical perspective on the theoretical direction of theory relating to supervision practice but also, as a consequence, suggests a novel approach to the delivery of supervision, effectively arguing for a clearer perspective on the association of supervisor and supervisee and a more positive and lucid paradigm in terms of the educational function and purpose of the supervisor.

Buber (1970) states that there are two ways of being-in-relation: I-Thou and I-It. The I-Thou, or dialogical, mode of relating is necessary for authentic being: it is momentary, and cannot be consciously brought about, although there are preconditions and factors that encourage dialogue. The meeting of I and Thou takes place between two whole beings: the I-It relation (not a fully dialogical situation) can never do so. Each I-It relation holds the potential to become an I-Thou encounter, and – although the meeting of I and Thou cannot be sustained – every I-Thou encounter has a residual humanising effect on the participants (Guilherme and Morgan, 2009). It is this I-Thou encounter that supervision might, at its best, achieve.

Knowledge is at root neither subjective nor objective, but essentially dialogical (Friedman, 2002): only in the meeting between I and Thou is one vulnerable to the irreducible uniqueness of the present and the whole reality of the other. I-It relations are always necessarily experienced through pre-existing categories and patterns of thought.

I-It relations involve experiencing, using or knowing some object. They sustain us, fulfilling our basic needs and desires as material entities (Guilherme and Morgan, 2009). I-Thou encounters cannot sustain, but do provide a glance toward the absolute and to eternity. One must recognise the distinction between I-Thou and I-It in order to avoid manipulating others (Buber, in Friedman, 1964).

The chapter looks at four themes that are present in Buber's educational philosophy, and that are of relevance to the practice of supervision. In each case, the Buberian approach is contrasted with a feasible alternative perspective. The first theme concerns the principal purpose of supervision. Kadushin and Harkness (2002) suggest that the primary purpose of supervision is to ensure the efficiency and effectiveness of services to clients. This is achieved through the overlapping and interrelated administrative, educative and supportive functions of supervision. The administrative function of supervision is the 'systematic coordination of effort in order that the objectives of the group are to be efficiently accomplished' (Kadushin and Harkness, 2002: 45). The educative function of supervision assists the supervisee in making 'the transition from knowing to doing' (ibid: 130). Educative supervision complements the training and formal education that the supervisee has received. While such courses are 'context-free and concerned with practice in general', in educative supervision the supervisor:

> . . . will reinforce, individualise, and demonstrate the applicability of the more general content taught in planned, formal in-service training sessions.
>
> Kadushin and Harkness, 2002: 131

The supportive function of supervision aims to decrease the supervisee's job-related stress and increase their motivation and commitment.

Buber's educational philosophy contends that direct knowing and real living are only possible through dialogue. Hence, a Buberian approach to supervision focuses on encouraging dialogue between supervisor and supervisee, with the primary purpose of developing the capacity of the supervisee to engage in dialogue more widely. This approach recognises the inherent value of enhancing skills, encouraging the supervisee to achieve their potential, supporting the supervisee, and helping them deal with stress. However, a Buberian approach insists that readiness for, and openness to, dialogue must remain the primary purpose of education. Supervision that excludes this possibility – and is entirely focused on personal development, achieving objectives and providing support – leads to individualisation and alienation.

The second theme concerns authority in supervision. Buber states that it is necessary for the educator to accept their authority without becoming authoritarian: Kadushin and Harkness (2002) note that, in practice, supervisors are often reluctant to use their authority. Authors on supervision tend to support the constructive use of authority in supervision, but acknowledge that the idea of authority is often perceived as being immiscible with the values of social work or with voluntary sector values (Clarke, 1997).

Buber (1997) describes two approaches to authority in educative association, where the educator is likened to a gardener and a sculptor respectively. Buber advocates a combination of the authority and discipline intrinsic to the sculptor with the active life and hope affirming characteristics that are found in the gardener (these metaphors will be elaborated on later).

Kadushin and Harkness (2002) consider that the authority of the supervisor comes from their position within the employing agency. Buber insists that the authority of the educator derives from:

- The example they set.
- The relationship of dialogue within the educative encounter.
- The capability of the educator to encourage wider engagement in dialogue.

Buber's concept of confirmation comprises accepting the other as they are now and acknowledging their potential to grow and change. Confirmation is possible through the formative and influential role of the educator, and through dialogue between educator and student.

Buber notes the limits of reciprocity that derive from the purposive nature of the educative association: between adults, there can be a more even reciprocity and more sharing of authority than would be the case in the education of children (Guilherme and Morgan, 2009). Hence in supervision, whilst the supervisor should acknowledge their authority, a high degree of mutuality is possible.

The third research theme concerns responsibility. Buber (2002) distinguishes between two possible approaches to determining how to act when situations present themselves. Using the first approach:

> . . . one can construct types of situations, one can always find to what section the particular situation belongs, and draw what is appropriate from the hoard of established maxims and habits, apply the appropriate maxim, bring into operation the appropriate habit.

> Buber, 2002: 134–5

Buber (2002: 135) criticises this approach, suggesting that untypical features of the present situation will go unnoticed. He likens situations that arise to newborn babies, in that each deserves a particular response that recognises its uniqueness. Despite apparent similarities:

> . . . every living situation has, like a newborn child, a new face, that has never been seen before and will never come again. It demands of you a reaction that cannot be prepared beforehand. It demands nothing of what is past. It demands presence, responsibility; it demands you.

Buber demands more than reflection: indeed he all but names reflection as, of itself inadequate to the task of comprehension and understanding.

Hence, responsibility is the ability to respond to the uniqueness of the situation that presents itself. Rules are still of value, as 'no responsible person remains a stranger to norms', but 'maxims command only the third person, the each and the none' (Buber, 2002: 135–6). As Friedman (2002: 240) notes:

> . . . traditional values are useful and suggestive, but one may not for all that proceed from them to the situation. Rather one must move from the concrete situation to the decision as to what is the right direction in this instance.

Hence, one must choose between the 'once-for-all of general moral norms' and the insecurity of openness and responding to 'the unique and irreducible situation to which no general categories could ever do justice' (Friedman, 1988: 152). This has particular resonance for those working within many contemporary organisations where policies and procedures are often composed with the intention of prescribing the required course of action in a range of circumstances. In policy statements, situations are often categorised – with appropriate steps and actions ascribed to each grouping. There is increasing competition between service providers for contracts with external funding bodies: these contracts frequently stipulate in detail the outputs to be measured.

The fourth theme concerns the example of the supervisor. Buberian dialogue between people requires the full presence of each 'Only in his whole being, in all his spontaneity can the educator truly affect the whole being of his pupil' (Buber, 2002: 125).

Supervision, in contrast, has been described as a relationship between roles, not people (Christian and Kitto, 1987). The concept of role seems predicated on the idea that an individual's life can be separated into sets of expectations and requirements. Hence, certain attitudes and behaviours are expected at work, but outside of work different criteria may apply. Buber insists that it is impossible to educate others in values that you are not living yourself. For Buber, the educator must set an example, and the example is the whole of their life.

The primary purpose of supervision

This section will contrast the distinction between the view that the primary purpose of supervision is to increase the effectiveness of the supervisee through developing their skills and the Buberian perspective, that the supervisor's ability to indicate the possibilities for dialogue is of primary importance.

The purpose of educative encounters such as supervision can be described in terms of gaining particular knowledge, techniques, skills or competencies – either for a specific purpose, such as a work role, or more generally for the fulfilment of potential. However, supervision, as a site of education might be expected to be more than a locale or process for the transmission of information or the development of proficiency.

Education

Albert Einstein famously had it that 'education is what remains after one has forgotten everything learned in school'. He also had it that imagination was more important than knowledge when it came understanding the workings of the universe. While gaining knowledge and skills is important, education that exclusively considers the development of potential, may lead to individualisation and alienation. Despite the necessarily concise and sometimes trite dictionary definitions of the word 'education', the activity has, across borders and over time, been understood as an experience that arises out of purposeful, conscious, collaborative activity (educational labour). Yes, you might find observing someone digging a hole provides some information or guidance about hole digging, or one might recall a pithy saying about liberty repeated by a grandparent that has been something of a guiding principal in one's life. However, these influences are not necessarily educational, although they may involve the accumulation of knowledge or cause one to think and, together with education, be part of what leads one to the getting of wisdom.

For instance, Fred read a book about dog racing and felt he had been informed by it. His previous knowledge of dog racing had been enhanced or confirmed. When Freda asked him about the book he was quick to tell her about what he had learnt. She listened intently. He had a smug smile on his face when he had finished because he felt sure he was now much more educated about dog racing than Freda. However, Freda wanted more than information as she, based on her knowledge of dog racing, had always believed it to be cruel and what Fred had told her just confirmed that belief. So she gave Fred information that explained why she thought dog racing was cruel. Fred had never seen dog racing as cruel, and there had been nothing in his dog racing book about this, so when Freda told him why she thought what he saw as a fine sport was in fact no more than a callous form of public amusement, he (like her) wanted more than information. At this point they were both ready for an educative encounter:

- The exploration and questioning of each others opinions, knowledge and ideas.
- A mutual analysis and comparison of their individual and shared knowledge.
- An argument about the place, purpose, conduct of a particular activity.

If both Freda and Fred enter into this association with relatively open minds, ready to be collaborative, generous, affably argumentative and assertive, rather than dogmatic, selfish, defensive, violent and stubborn, their individual knowledge and perceptions might develop. It will not be about 'winning', or one being proved more 'right' than the other. In the best of all possible worlds each will generate a different perception about dog racing because a dialectic would have occurred rather than a mere conversation or chat.

However, because Fred or Freda successfully enter into an educative association does not mean they are educators, just as fixing the washer on a tap does not make one a plumber; one act of plumbing does not a plumber make, and one educative encounter does not make one an educator.

Fred and Freda could have read other books, watched television programmes or films, gone to the theatre and picked up a book and entered into an educative encounter with the author or a playwright and so on (although this might have been less obvious). However, the idea that everyone is and always will be an educator (as some writers on informal education argue) is flawed. If every colour is blue, there are no colours, not even blue, because blue can only be named as blue in relation to that which is not blue. Likewise if everything is education nothing is education. That is why it might be argued that claims that most experience, or even all experience, is educational are in fact the proclamation of ignorance about the nature and process of education.

Driving instructors are not called 'driving educators' as it is not the role of the driving instructor to do more than effectively pass on skill and information about driving. They are unlikely to prioritise promoting arguments with their clients, for example about why driving exists, if it is a good or bad thing to stop at a red light etc. The primary task of a tour guide is to guide tours, show where places are and provide more or less what are the agreed facts about those places. They are not 'tour educators'; in the main they are not really interested in, or keen to enter into a debate focused on alternative understandings of their knowledge and perceptions about their tours. If you don't believe this, when you are next involved with a guided tour, try questioning the guide, suggesting they might have the wrong end of the proverbial stick. Is it probable the more you question the less they will value your patronage? This does not mean that tour guides or driving instructions might not from time to time enter into educative associations with others, much like Freda and Fred. But also like Fred and Freda this will not make them educators per se.

So what's happening?

Supervision is often conceptualised in terms of developing potential, gaining insight or awareness. However, Sawdon and Sawdon (1995: 3) discuss the need to foster the personal resources of workers 'in the interests of effective service delivery'. In contrast, Buber refers to dialogue being both at the heart of the process and as the primary purpose of education. Hence, supervision – as an educative process – is both about and for dialogue that, in ideal circumstances, encompasses dialectic.

Definitions of supervision tend to focus either on the supervisee, or on the work itself (Christian and Kitto, 1987, and Kadushin and Harkness, 2002 for example). The distinction may be slight as Christian and Kitto add that the worker remains fully responsible for the work. But the issue remains as to whether it is the worker, who is responsible for the work, or the work itself that is at the centre of supervision.

However, the character of supervision does risk drawing the supervisee into introspection, or perhaps some might say obsession with self. But it is not for our own sakes that we practice. This might suggest that the focus of supervision should be on the worker for the sake of the work. For Buber however, at the heart of any educative relationship is the dialogue between the participants. So from this perspective supervision will be centred on the dialogue between supervisor and supervisee, in order to develop the supervisee's capacity to bring about and respond to dialogue in work and life.

In 1923, Buber was invited to address an international education conference in Heidelberg: the topic that he was given was 'The Development of the Creative Powers of the Child' (Buber, 2002a: 98). The address is widely considered of great importance to educational theory, partly because existential philosophy was applied to the field of education for the first time (Weinstein, 1975). Buber stated in his address that he did not consider the task of education involved either development or creative powers. As Clarke (1946: 64) notes:

> *The address must have surprised his audience, for he begins by rejecting the idea of creativeness as a human trait and prefers to speak of man as originator or producer.*

Buber argued that people cannot create, but can form and transform creation through instincts for origination and communion (Weinstein, 1975: 134). The instinct for origination is important in education, but is not the primary focus of education because it cannot lead to dialogue. Therefore:

Through this instinct we learn how to form things and how to put them together . . .
Yet, the instinct of origination cannot teach us the being of the world and the
viaticum of life which are at the heart and core of education.

So the instinct for origination is our drive to express ourselves, to experiment and solve
problems. The instinct for communion, or authentic human relationship, 'is the kernel
of education and its process is dialogue' (Weinstein, 1975: 35). So education concerns
co-operation and involvement with others, through dialogue.

For Buber, the primary function of education is the 'nurturing of relational capacities,
rather than the provision of opportunities for self-expression and [individual] growth'
(Murphy, 1988: 92). So, Buber's critique of the emphasis on individual creative potential
in education is grounded in his philosophy of the primacy of dialogue over experience.
It is not as creators, but as fellow creatures that we encounter each other in dialogue.
Therefore, education solely focused on developing creative potential leads to individualisation and alienation. The instinct to originate must be met with education based on
dialogue through which it is transformed – because it is through authentic encounters
with nature and other people that the individual becomes fully human (Clarke, 1946).

Buber (2002a: 123) considers that any education 'worthy of the name' is education
of character:

Personality is something which in its growth remains essentially outside the
influence of the educator; but to assist in the moulding of character is his greatest
task.

Christian and Kitto (1987: 7) define supervision as:

. . . a process whereby one person enables another to think better . . . to . . . think
about the work, in such a way that it enables the worker to think better outside the
supervision session.

Thinking, in this definition, includes emotional, attitudinal, and motivational elements.
While endorsing the value of increasing the capacity of the worker to think, a model of
supervision grounded in Buber's thought needs to fully consider the role of dialogue.
The supervision relationship should be a process whereby supervisor and supervisee
engage in dialogue in such a way as to increase the supervisee's capacity for dialogue
with others and the world – starting with the supervisor.

Following Buber, supervision, as an educative interaction, has an overarching purpose
to improve the quality of service offered to clients. So, whilst incremental increases in
the skills and knowledge of the supervisee may lead directly to benefits for clients – the
process of supervision must always return to the wider possibilities for dialogue. If it is
exclusively through dialogical encounters with the world – and especially with other
people – that real living is found and direct knowledge is possible, then the supervision
relationship needs to model the relationships that are possible with clients.

Hence the cultivation of dialogue is both an essential element in the process of
supervision, and the primary purpose of supervision: rather than focusing solely on the

growth and development of the worker, the supervisor should seek to develop the supervisee's capacity for dialogue, within – and especially beyond – the association of supervision.

Authority in educational encounters

Buber states that educative encounters require a trusting mutuality, but notes the limits of reciprocity in education. The authority of the teacher, or supervisor, is derived from the example they set; from the relationship of dialogue that is education and from the ability of the educator to point to greater opportunities for dialogue. In practice however, many supervisors are disinclined to assert their authority, preferring to promote a more egalitarian encounter.

In relation to notions of authority, Buber (1997) acknowledges two prevailing approaches in education: in the first, the educator is likened to a gardener; in the second approach the educator is compared to a sculptor. The gardening metaphor sees the educator bringing out of the student that which the student already possesses, albeit in latent form. The objective of such education is to develop what is inherent – to permit students to become themselves. The sculptor, in contrast, has an image in mind – according to which the student is to be shaped. The problem facing the sculptor is that 'even the most distinguished educator cannot create a truly valid ideal' from which to begin fashioning the student (Buber, 1997, p.150). So the gardener exercises authority only insofar as to enable development and flourishing, whereas the sculptor influences others to a much greater extent.

Kadushin and Harkness (2002: 131) note that two of the strongest sources of satisfaction amongst social work supervisors are 'helping the supervisee grow and develop as a professional' and 'satisfaction in sharing social work knowledge and skills': these correspond in part to the gardener and sculptor models of education respectively.

Power and freedom

A common criticism of supervision practice that might be seen as akin to the gardening metaphor is that the supervisor is often passive, acting as a 'sounding board' or slavishly following a version of the Socratic Method. In such situations the supervisee is thought to be obliged to rely on their own initiative and capabilities. Christian and Kitto (1987: 6) respond by arguing that the seemingly flaccid supervisor is in reality working to 'facilitate the worker's thinking'. This might be all very well if the supervisee is relatively professionally competent, but it cuts down the potential of the supervision as a site of critique and, if necessitated, professional guidance.

Buber sees the authentic educator taking a formative and purposeful role that involves the avoidance authoritarianism, while fostering dialogue. Here the supervisor is a largely benign but active presence, operating on their own integrity, with a focused coherence with intentions, words and actions aligned.

Supervision practice has also been criticised on the grounds that relate to the sculptor metaphor. This critique is built around the accusation that authority is held almost exclusively by the supervisor, with the supervisee having to disclose information about the work, whether they want to or not (Christian and Kitto, 1987). This criticism is rooted in an understanding of authority as inferring an absence of freedom. Christian and Kitto (1987) respond that the supervisee has the freedom to choose how best to make use of the supervision session, and that the supervisor has the freedom to choose how to respond. Buber is critical of this notion of freedom as the opposite of compulsion, or merely the absence of external constraint. He argues that freedom of choice has been conflated with freedom for self-expression and growth, with the result that freedom is perceived as an important end in itself (Murphy, 1988). For Buber, however, freedom is a precondition for dialogue, and he comments:

> *Freedom in education is the possibility of communion ... without it nothing succeeds, but neither does anything succeed by means of it: it is the run before the jump, the tuning of the violin.*
>
> Buber, 2002a: 108

So freedom is the prerequisite for communion in education: although a necessary foundation, it is not active in the process towards dialogue. The distinction between this and the position espoused by Christian and Kitto (1987) is fine, but whilst Christian and Kitto perceive a role for freedom of choice in the ongoing process of supervision, Buber states that it is an essential prerequisite, not an active ingredient. Buber promotes a 'formative, disciplinary and highly purposive role for the teacher, in opposition to 'sentimentalised, child-indulging tendencies' typical in the gardening approach to education (Murphy, 1988: 94; 93). Hence Buber asserts the necessity of the educator having authority, without becoming authoritarian. He recommends a combination of the authority and discipline inherent in the sculpting approach to education, with the dynamic, life and hope affirming qualities ingrained in the gardening approach (Murphy, 1988). The authority of the educator cannot be based on objective categories of knowledge. The moral authority of the teacher:

> *... is grounded in the integrity and truth of the relation in which the teacher is reciprocally engaged with his pupils and by the various forms of relational truth towards which he can guide them by his word and example.*
>
> Murphy, 1988: 95

So the authority of the supervisor is anchored by both the relationship of dialogue between supervisor and supervisee, and in the attempts the supervisor makes to point towards the wider possibilities for dialogue.

Stanners (1995) recommends definitions of supervision that focus on the reciprocity of the relationship, rather than notions of control. Kadushin and Harkness (2002) also note reluctance amongst supervisors to use the power and authority available to them. They suggest that this may be partly owing to the perception that the exercise of power and authority is ideologically antithetical to the values of social work practice – such as the emphasis on mutual, egalitarian and noncoercive relationships. Clarke (1997: 2) notes that this applies to the voluntary sector as well, where 'supervision is generally associated with inspection, control, overseeing, hierarchy and often as just a matter of checking on work and giving instructions'.

Clarke suggests that supervision can be used to empower and motivate staff. Kadushin and Harkness (2002: 99) note that the functional necessity of exercising power to ensure organisational objectives are met is inextricably bound up with emotions of 'prestige, self-esteem, superiority, inferiority, dominance and submission'. Sawdon and Sawdon (1995: 9) suggest, however, that the:

> . . . effective supervisor does not deny her/his power and authority but uses it to ensure with the supervisee that s/he is clear about what is required and how they are meeting or not meeting those requirements together.

Hewson (1999) notes that, in feminist discourse, power is often perceived as being entirely negative and destructive. She suggests that, owing to this, some feminist supervisors endeavour to establish 'friendly and equal supervisory relationships'. However, she asserts that attempts to create egalitarianism in supervision may inadvertently intensify the power of the supervisor, increasing the potential for 'subtle abuse':

> . . . since the supervisory relationship is not structurally egalitarian, an overtly egalitarian relationship simply submerges the structural power as a covert force. When power is not permitted to be recognised or named, it cannot be negotiated or challenged.

> Ibid: 406

So, in apparently more egalitarian supervisory relationships authority is submerged rather than eliminated. Hawkins and Shohet (2000) – whilst recommending the appropriate use of power and authority by the supervisor – note that, in practice, supervisors often struggle with having power and authority. So whilst the authors do not generally espouse a view of the supervisory relationship based on equality of status rather than the presence of supervisor authority, they recognise that this does occur in practice. Arnett (1986: 143) suggests that a reluctance to use power often stems from:

> . . . a genuine and sincere conviction that people should be treated with a dignity that recognises responsibility for themselves; an attempt to aid others 'too much' is seen as an act of paternalism.

Arnett points out that such reluctance is ultimately rooted in an individualistic world view, which fails to recognise the people's interdependence. Kadushin and Harkness (2002: 85) distinguish between power and authority, stating:

> Authority is the right that legitimises the use of power; power is the ability to implement authority . . . The distinction is seen clearly in situations in which a person may have authority but no power to act, and vice versa.

Kadushin and Harkness (2002) give two examples to illustrate the distinction – a hijacker, and a prison warden held hostage by prisoners. The former has great power but not authority, the latter has authority but no power to act. Kadushin and Harkness (2002: 84) note that authority is essential for the formation of a supervisory relationship:

The supervisory relationship is established through authority delegated to the supervisor by the agency and through the supervisee's reciprocal acceptance of the supervisor's legitimate entitlement to authority.

Buber does not accept that the authority of the supervisor is derived from an entitlement external to the supervision relationship: the supervisor's position within the organisational hierarchy may provide them with power, but their authority is grounded in dialogue, and in the example they provide. Buber accepted authority when the situation made it appropriate to do so:

If a person came to Buber for counselling, he did not try to act as if he were not an authority figure. He allowed himself to be viewed as a leader in a situation in which his counsel and judgement were sought out.

Arnett, 1986: 152

The educative function of supervision often involves the consideration of professional judgements. The supervisee brings to the meeting the various matters and questions that they have prepared for discussion with their supervisor. In circumstances where the supervisor then answers each point from their existing repertoire of professional knowledge, there can be no dialogue. Instead, the supervisor must be willing to have their beliefs and attitudes tested: Arnett (1986: 152) notes that Buber was willing to persuade a partner in dialogue, only 'as he was simultaneously willing to be persuaded'. It is this commitment to the potential for revision of previous held ideas and positions that keeps alive the possibility of dialogue:

In dialogue, each individual must be willing to let the other's stance challenge his or her own, to test ideas, while still affirming the personhood of the challenger.

Arnett, 1986: 152

From their ability to inspire and encourage this meeting in dialogue, where the pertinent matters from the supervisee's practice are discussed, the authority of the supervisor is derived.

For Buber, power is a 'social phenomenon between persons and events that is unavoidable and inevitable' (Arnett, 1986: 147). Additionally, Buber does not perceive power as harmful or destructive:

Power is intrinsically guiltless and is the precondition for the actions of man. It is the will to power, the greed for more power than others, which is destructive . . . Not renunciation of power but responsibility in the exercise of power prevents it from becoming evil.

Friedman, 2002: 51

So the supervisor must exercise the power they have; their duties, authority and responsibly, rather than abandoning or relinquishing it. The responsible use of power encourages dialogue:

Buber was concerned that the power to manipulate and use another increases with a decrease in the power to enter into relation.

Arnett, 1986: 145

Friedman (2002: 208) notes that the teacher needs to 'see the position of the other in his concrete actuality yet does not lose sight of his own'. The pupil, in contrast, cannot inhabit the situation from the perspective of the educator:

The educator stands at both ends of the common situation, the pupil only at one end. In the moment when the pupil is able to throw himself across and experience from over there, the educative relation would be burst asunder, or change into friendship.

Buber, 2002a: 119

The educative relationship, according to Buber, is one of trusting mutuality – which is based on inclusion but cannot constitute inclusion because 'if it loses one-sidedness it loses essence' (Buber, 2002a: 117). Hence, there are limits to the reciprocity possible in the teacher-student relationship. But this need not prevent the supervisee teaching the supervisor about their situation or perspective. Indeed while the emphasis is on the supervisee to learn, they must also be ready to teach; likewise while the supervisor role might be premised on education, part of this is a willingness to learn. This mutuality might be understood as a central trait that marks out the nature of dialogue.

It is the purposive nature of the supervisory association that prevents the unfolding of full mutuality, a 'normative limitation' that the teacher shares with the psychotherapist and the pastor (Buber, 2004: 99) and probably also the social and youth worker. Guilherme and Morgan (2009: 569) state that from Buber's perspective '. . . it makes complete sense to talk about a dialogical relation that is one-sided inclusive within the educational realm . . .' But this allows for, '. . . various levels, shades and hues of inclusion'.

Mutuality and change

Guilhermen and Morgan make the point that the relationship with a lover may be more intense than with a friend, and that the mutuality with a close relation is more inclusive than with a student. However, they suggest that adult education allows for greater mutuality than would be appropriate in the education of children. So between adults, the educative relationship can be 'more symmetrically reciprocal and more empowering' (Guilherme and Morgan, 2009: 570). In his detailed treatment of the mutuality possible in helping relationships, Berry (1985: 67) states that the normative limitation to which Buber refers 'attaches to the relationship, not the relation as such'. In this way, the full relation of dialogue is possible in education, even as the particular nature of the relationship limits reciprocity.

Murphy (1988) suggests that the relationship between educator and student constantly aspires towards dialogue. He suggests that Buber intends a counselling role for the educator, particularly in order to help the students find meaning in times characterised by 'moral uncertainty, social alienation, the decline of faith, [and] the diminished status of cultural traditions' (Murphy, 1988: 101). Within this therapeutic function, adopted by the educator, are the concepts of confirmation and acceptance.

For Murphy (1988) Buber distinguishes between acceptance and confirmation, but that ultimately acceptance is included in his concept of confirmation. It seems clear from the transcript of Buber's famous 1957 moderated public dialogue with Carl Rogers, that Buber's concept of confirmation of future potential includes accepting a person as they are now (Anderson and Cissna, 1997).

In the dialogue with Rogers, Buber notes that accepting somebody as they are now does not necessarily exclude wanting them to change. He comments:

> . . . take, for example, eh a man and a woman, man and wife. And eh he says, not expressly, but just by his whole relation to her, eh 'I accept you as you are.' But this does not mean 'I don't want you to change.' But it eh says, 'I discover in you, just by my accepting love, I eh discover in you what you are meant to become.' Eh, this is, of course, not anything to be eh expressed in missive terms.
>
> Buber, in Anderson and Cissna, 199: 91

So, from this example, Buber's concept of confirmation implies an acknowledgement of potential to grow and change. Buber also includes the possibility of specific knowledge of that potential.

Acceptance is to acknowledge the other as they are now: confirmation is 'the overall process that includes the possibility of affecting the potential of the other' (Anderson and Cissna, 1997: 92). There is also a sense in the passage of how confirmation is expressed. In the example, the man conveys confirmation through his whole relation to his wife, not through verbal expression. Anderson and Cissna (1997) suggest two levels of meaning in Buber's use of the phrase 'missive terms': firstly he was reinforcing the idea that confirmation is demonstrated in practice rather than being articulated in speech; secondly, he is calling to mind the nuance of officialdom in the term 'missive' to declare that confirmation cannot be demanded or enforced. Murphy (1988) declares that Buber's concept of confirmation is grounded in his view of the role of the educator as formative and influential. He notes that:

> The influencing he describes, however, is one which remains rooted in the trust, the personal exemplification of integrity and the pastoral counselling concern that have been identified as the essential characteristics of the teacher.
>
> Murphy, 1988: 103

So Buber's approach to learning and knowing entails a collaborative effort by educator and students in which the students determine for themselves the personal significance of the world as they encounter it (Murphy, 1988). The teacher is an educational motivator, structuring this encounter for educative effect. This can be replicated in the supervisory association.

Buber, supervision and authority in summary

Applying Buber's argument, that the educator should accept their authority without becoming authoritarian, to the educative encounter of supervision, the Buberian supervisor acknowledges their authority which is grounded in their ability to encourage dialogue. Many authors interested in supervision agree that supervisors should use their authority constructively, but recognise that – in practice – supervisors are often reluctant to accept or use their authority. Kadushin and Harkness (2002) state that the authority of the supervisor derives from their position within the agency: Buberian authority derives from the dialogical relation between supervisor and supervisee, and the competence of the supervisor in indicating the wider possibilities for dialogue. Writers examining supervision have recognised that supervisors within the helping professions are often more comfortable establishing an egalitarian relationship with their supervisees, although they caution against this (for example Hewson, 1999). Buber concurs, stating that the purposive nature of such a relationship necessarily imposes a normative constraint on reciprocity. Aligned with the Buberian approach to authority is his concept of confirmation: rather than merely accepting someone as they are, confirmation also implies recognising their potential to grow and change. Hence, a Buberian supervisor would accept a formative and influential role – not as an entitlement derived from their position in an organisation's hierarchy but originating from their dialogical relation with the supervisee.

Responsibility in the educative relationship

The concept of responsibility is at the heart of Buber's approach to education. Responsibility, or the ability to respond authentically to the current situation, entails making a decision rather than applying a principle. This does not exclude values from education, but it does require that they are not held inflexibly, regardless of the situation that presents itself. Trust – which is an important element of Buber's philosophy – is given as an example of such a value: maintaining the importance of trust in education does not engender particular actions regardless of context and therefore allows for genuine responding in a given situation.

Relationship and trust

A recent advertising campaign by Wiltshire Farm Foods claimed that the company was about 'friendship, reliability and nutrition'. In their promotion they claimed to develop relationships and trust with their clients. However, the company does not exist for such purposes, although they might *use* these sentiments. Their primary function is encapsulated via sales exceeding £70 million per year with a €500 million global turnover.

Likewise, the police force exists to uphold and enforce the law; whatever they do must serve this fundamental end. Faith organisations, those for instance affiliated to a particular church, will, in the last analysis, exist to promote and propagate ('spread the good news') of that branch of faith. If they did otherwise they would risk misappropriating the resources of the church donated by organisations and individuals to the 'cause of the church'. But it is likely that both the police and the church might claim they *use* trust and relationship-building in the pursuit of their primary tasks.

A faith organisation and the police force will come together when each party sees such a course as serving their primary functions. That is why a faith organisation might not accept donations from a casino or readily enter into a practice partnership with Spearmint Rhino. However, a faith organisation that is against the random use of drugs, violent crime or prostitution might well see the police as a potentially helpful/supportive partner.

The police and the faith organisation are each looking to promote conformity (to the law/religious belief) and to this extent they are both interested in control. With this in mind, why would the educational organisation be involved in the same sort of pursuit in respect of relationships and trust-building? Is not the educational organisation in our society a means to promote social conformity? All these organisations might claim to use 'trust' and the building of relationships (like Wiltshire Farm Foods) but those considerations are not what they exist for or the likely foundation of a partnership or collaboration between them (else they would be in partnership with the likes of Wiltshire Farm Foods).

A fundamental commonality between the educational organisation's function (its primary task) and the other social institutions is that the *use* of trust and relationship building is explicit. Put another way, as the state dictates what the police do and the faith community and the hierarchy of the church prescribes what the faith organisation does, so government policy directs the educational organisation's activity (it also directly/indirectly funds these organisations). This appears to include the instrumental and purposeful attempts to gain and use trust, via the fabrication of relationships. As such the idea of a relationship and the notion of trust are not, when deployed for mechanistic educational ends, what they might be taken to be when referred to in the general sense: they are tools, a means to an operational end and not part of mundane sensitivity and the relatively random stream of human interaction; they are consciously implicated into a professional strategy to promote institutionally desired change and/or prescribed social conformity

The instrumental approach has been made more obvious by the prevailing approach to the management of education, which is based on standards, targets and outcomes. Riley (1995) notes that this has been a result of a combination of legislation, increasing consumerism, and changes in management education. She notes that 'outcome cannot be assessed unless standards are set' (Riley, 1995, p.41). As McHenry (1997: 346–7) laments:

> . . . *from calls for measured improvement on standardised tests at the stages of a standard curriculum to computerised classrooms . . . we teachers may often be led to make do with the things that we experience and use . . . Even if we are not tied to a textbook's structure of information, or to a curriculum guide, we may find ourselves in the It-predicament. For we are led into It by our vocabulary, the conversation of our culture.*

Here, McHenry (1997: 347) identifies the 'objectivising, structurising' approach to education. In contrast to McHenry's description, Buber insists upon an approach where professionals maintain a responsibility to attend to each situation afresh and to act accordingly. Rather than relying on standards or principles that can be applied across a range of circumstances, the educator fosters dialogue by maintaining the ability to respond to the presenting particular situation. Thus:

> *There is not and never has been a norm and fixed maxim of education. What is called so was always only the norm of a culture, of a society, a church, an epoch.*
>
> Buber, 2002a: 120

Buber abjures principles for living, insisting that educators discover for themselves the required course of action in a given set of circumstances. This might be recognised as the honing of professional judgement:

> *I have no rigid principles. There is what has to be done here and now. I have only a direction and my senses, and I act according to the situation.*
>
> Buber, in Hodes, 1972: 218–19

Buber states that the educator must be aware of their environment, of the particular and specific circumstances and conditions in which they are living. In eschewing principles, Buber seeks to establish the necessity for the educator of interpreting for themselves 'how to live now' (ibid: 219). For Buber, adopting a principle for living implies a commitment to act in a prescribed manner regardless of the circumstances: this is always a mistake, however well-intentioned. Hence, when Buber is asked 'is 'help your comrade' a principle?' he replies, 'if you turn this into a principle, you will be wrong' (op. cit.: 219). It is important to note the sense of agency in Buber's reply: the problem comes not with valuing the idea expressed in 'help your comrade' – but with choosing to adopt this idea as a principle for living, to be applied regardless of context. This application of ideas into principles creates dogmas, whereas Buber insists, 'you must weigh things anew every time' (op. cit.: 219). As such, just accepting trust as a given, in terms of its 'purity' or how it is used, is 'wrong'. What trust is, is shaped by the environment in which it emerges. This does not necessarily prevent trust in the dialogical situation, but in the education encounters it is probably not a bad practice to be aware how trust can be 'used' in order to be better able to pursue the authentic trust which Buber promotes.

Buber seems aware of the challenge and responsibility this places on the shoulders of the educator: when he is asked 'what shall I judge by?' he replies 'By the situation and the way you see it. I am sorry. I cannot make it any easier for you' (ibid: 219).

For Buber, responsibility entails attending carefully to the here and now, and responding 'from the ground of one's being' (Friedman, 2002: 108):

> *Genuine responsibility exists only where there is real responding. Responding to what? To what happens to one, to what is seen and heard and felt.*
>
> Buber, 2002a: 18–19

Responsibility does not preclude membership of a group or community, but it is essential that no individual or association be allowed to inhibit either one's awareness of the 'unreduced claim of each particular hour in all its crudeness and disharmony', or one's authentic response (Friedman, 2002: 108).

It is important to note Buber's use of the term principle here: a principle is a tenet or doctrine that governs future behaviour regardless of the concrete situation. When Buber speaks – for example – of the necessity of trust in the educative relationship, this does not constitute the establishment of a principle because endorsing trust as a value does not stipulate or determine future behaviour. Hence Buber, in acknowledging the importance of hope for the practice of education, is not contradicting his stated aversion to principles:

> When I educate young people, I try to explain to them that there are things for which it is worth living. A real educator has an influence even without speaking.
>
> Buber, in Hodes, 1972: 219

Buber is emphatic regarding the value of trust: the educator must believe in the student and treat them with trust as prerequisites for dialogue between them. 'The first necessity is that the teacher must arouse in his pupils that most valuable thing of all – genuine trust' (Buber, in Hodes, 1972: 217).

For Buber, trust implies that 'something is given to the other, a challenge one has to take care of or refuse to do' (Kristiansen, 1996, p. 218). Trust involves the educator fully engaging in the situation, so trust comes directly from dialogue:

> The relation in education is one of pure dialogue ... trust, trust in the world, because this human being exists – that is the most inward achievement of the relation in education.
>
> Buber, 2002a: 116

Trust requires the real presence of the educator. This does not entail being continually concerned with the pupil, but there must be mutuality between them. In discussing the need to inspire courage in young people to 'break ... [the] spell' of considering themselves primarily to merely be objects of reality, Buber declares 'How does one educate for courage? Through nourishing trust. How does one nourish trust? Through one's own trustworthiness' (Buber, in Friedman, 1964: 63).

A philosophy that values dialogue, hope and trust can still encompass the need to evaluate each situation in its particularity without contradiction. Similarly, agency values – such as treating each other with respect – do not tend to prescribe behaviour across numerous situations with any great precision. However, rules such as those concerning confidentiality, are often formulated in great detail with the specific intention of creating a clear set of principles, covering all foreseeable circumstances and leaving as little room for interpretation as possible. Buber holds that objective knowledge should be brought back into the specific encounter that presents itself. Hence, agency policies and rules are valuable – but need to inform the dialogue rather than being applied mechanistically. The distinction here is one of intention: policies are often deliberately written in such a way as to ensure a consistent, standardised approach regardless of particular circumstances.

Buber's philosophy of dialogue requires that room be left for responsibility – the ability to respond to what is seen, heard and felt. As Friedman (1996: x) explains:

> *Structure is necessary as well as spontaneity, as Buber says repeatedly – not just any structure, however, but structure that makes spontaneity possible, planning that leaves room for surprises.*

As such, the Buberian view can be understood to posit that structure, albeit necessary, and must leave space for people to be able to respond authentically to the particular circumstances that confront them at any given time. This insight applies to the conduct of supervision itself, and to the supervisor's representation of organisational policies, culture and practices to the supervisee. The organisation that constructs a prescriptive framework of policies and procedures with the intention of ensuring a consistent approach across a range of situations risks inhibiting the responsibility – or ability to respond – of their professional staff. As such it can often inhibit the development of professional judgement.

However, given the current weight of bureaucratic, administrative and instrumental expectations of practice, the practitioner would be justified to ask how a Buberian approach to supervision might be overtly implemented. But because the environment is difficult might not be sufficient reason for supervisors to fail to seek to implement the most effective methodology in relation to their client's professional needs.

The example of the educator

Being a supervisor is often described as a role that can be contrasted with other roles within the 'caring' professions (Kadushin and Harkness, 2002, for example). Hawkins and Shohet (2000) note that different roles encompass different expectations: for instance, one expects diagnosis from a doctor. Importance is therefore attached to defining the roles of supervisor and supervisee, in order to ensure that their relationship is coherently supervisory, rather than becoming more akin to another role within the helping professions such as therapy or counselling.

Supervision is thus often perceived as a relationship between roles, rather than people. 'Supervision . . . is about a role not a person, and the working relationship is one between the holders of two particular roles' (Christian and Kitto, 1987: 12).

The relationship of dialogue, however, is always between whole beings. The concept of role separates out an individual's life into sets of requirements for different circumstances. Thus, a certain demeanour and patterns of behaviour are expected at work, for example – but one is free to adopt quite a different role once home. In contrast to this, Buber sees an educator as leading by example – and the example is the whole of their life:

Everything depends on the teacher as a man, as a person. He educates from himself, from his virtues and faults, through personal example and according to the circumstances and conditions.

Buber, in Hodes, 1972: 146

Discussing Buber's educational spirit, Gordon (1973: 222) declares the necessity of relating to the whole person:

Realising this spirit in education implies more than suggesting a behavioural-humanistic-model or seeking out other human beings as a holiday task. It means that the educator's whole existence should be impregnated by the feeling that we can humanise the world by relating.

Buber is often referred to as an existentialist and Friedman (2002: 190) notes 'In existential thinking man vouches for his word with his life and stakes his life in his thought'.

Buber is recognised as having achieved such a unity of thought and life (Friedman, 2002, for example). Yet he, in common with many thinkers, regarded labels – such as existentialism – with some disdain. Buber (2002a: 124) points to the importance of education that is grounded in the lives of students. He considers it a failure if, in his example, a child prone to lying produces a well-written report on the negative consequences of lying. Thus he demonstrates his regard for unity of life and thought.

In a conversation described in Hodes (1972) Buber is asked how to educate the children of the kibbutz to help each other and to value truth and justice. Buber replies:

As long as you do not recognise the roots of this problem in yourselves, how can you change it in your pupils? Every genuine action begins with a recognition of the historical truth – in other words, what has actually happened.

Buber, in Hodes, 1972: 216

So, in the spirit of dialogue, Buber offers a challenge to the members of the kibbutz: it is not possible to educate others in values that you are not living yourself. In *The Way of Man*, Buber considers the Hasidic story of a conversation between an imprisoned Zaddik (one who embodies the religious ideals of Judaism) and the police chief. The chief raises an apparent paradox in the Torah but 'the reply is given on a different plane from that on which the question is asked' (Buber, 2002: 4). The Zaddik's answer 'illuminates both the situation of the biblical Adam and that of every man in every time and place', and therefore has a personal message for the chief (ibid: 5). Something similar happens in the challenge that Buber offers during the dialogue with members of the kibbutz. Firstly, Buber points to a more general conclusion: that the authentic educator cannot dissociate their educative practice from the way in which they live. Thus, in his reply, Buber is speaking to all educators at all times. Buber also redirects the attention of the kibbutz members: 'the essential thing is to begin with oneself' (Buber, 2002b: 21).

The idea that teaching is a profession pursued by those unable to achieve in other fields of endeavour is one that has, to an extent, passed into received wisdom. Buber's writings stand in direct opposition to this idea: for example, his descriptions of Hasidic teachers (Zaddikim) demonstrate an essential unity of life and teaching (Buber, 2002b). Far from envisioning teaching because one cannot do, Buber's vision of the teacher is of one who cannot teach until they can do – through leading by example.

> *A zaddik ... was a teacher ... who taught as much by example as by word of mouth. One zaddik said of his own teacher: 'I learnt Torah from all my teacher's limbs.*

> Vermes, 1988: 17

Buber's position on teaching is much closer to that of Ghandi, whom he admired (Hodes, 1972, on their similarities). A story attributed to Ghandi relates to a woman who brings her son to see him in order for him to instruct the boy to stop eating sugar: Ghandi tells them to return in three weeks, during which time he stops eating sugar himself. Until he had achieved something himself, he was unwilling to instruct others to do otherwise. This has strong parallels with Buber's declaration that a teacher 'could not teach others if his own example was flawed' (Hodes, 1972: 137).

Hence the Buberian perspective is that the supervisor sets an example with the whole of their life: it is essential to live and teach with integrity – for words to be in accordance with actions. An alternative position is that nothing in the life of the supervisor outside of the work setting has any bearing on their ability to supervise or instruct.

In conclusion, the Buberian supervisor is focused on the possibility of dialogue in supervision, whilst pointing out the wider possibilities for dialogue. They accept a formative and purposive role in the supervision association but avoid authoritarianism. They plan and organise but are able to respond authentically to the particular parenting circumstances. They are able to integrate educative practises with their whole life.

References

Anderson, R. and Cissna, K.N. (1997) *The Martin Buber – Carl Rogers Dialogue: A New Transcript with Commentary*. State University of New York Press.

Arnett, R.C. (1986) *Communication and Community: Implications of Martin Buber's Dialogue*. Southern Illinois University Press.

Berry, D.L. (1985) *Mutuality: The Vision of Martin Buber*. State University of New York Press.

Buber, M. (1957) *Pointing the Way*. Routledge and Kegan Paul.

Buber, M. (1970) *I and Thou*. T. & T. Clark (W. Kaufmann translation).

Buber, M. (1997) *Israel and the World: Essays in a Time of Crisis*. Syracuse University Press.

Buber, M. (2002a) *Between Man and Man*. Routledge.

Buber, M. (2002b) *The Way of Man*. Routledge.

Buber, M. (2004) *I and Thou*. 2nd edn, Continuum (R.G. Smith Translation).

Christian, C. and Kitto, J. (1987) *The Theory and Practice of Supervision*. YMCA George Williams College.

Clarke, F. (1946) *Freedom in the Educative Society*. University of London Press.

Clarke, J. (1997) *Managing Better: Staff Support and Supervision*. Combat Poverty Agency.

Friedman, M. (1964) Interrogation of Martin Buber. In Rome, S. and Rome, B. (Eds.) *Philosophical Interrogations*. Holt, Rinehart and Winston.

Friedman, M. (1988) *Martin Buber's Life and Work: The Later Years 1945–1965*. Wayne State University Press.

Friedman, M. (1996) Foreword to the 1996 Edition. In Moore, D.J. *Martin Buber: Prophet of Religious Secularism*. 2nd edn, Fordham University Press.

Friedman, M. (2002) *Martin Buber: The Life of Dialogue*. 4th edn, Routledge.

Gordon, H. (1973) Would Martin Buber Endorse the Buber Model? *Educational Theory*, 23: 3, Summer.

Guilherme, A. and Morgan, W.J. (2009) Martin Buber's Philosophy of Education and its Implications for Adult Non-Formal Education. *International Journal of Lifelong Education*, 28: 5, 565–81.

Hawkins, P. and Shohet, R. (2000) *Supervision in the Helping Professions*. 2nd edn, Open University Press.

Hewson, D. (1999) III. Empowerment in Supervision. *Feminism & Psychology*, 9: 4, 406–9.

Hodes, A. (1972) *Encounter with Martin Buber*. Allen Lane The Penguin Press.

Kadushin, A. and Harkness, D. (2002) *Supervision in Social Work*. 4th edn, Columbia University Press.

Kristiansen, A. (1996) The Interhuman Dimension of Teaching: Some Ethical Aspects. In Friedman, M. (Ed.) *Martin Buber and the Human Sciences*. State University of New York Press.

McHenry, H.D. (1997) Education as Encounter: Buber's Pragmatic Ontology. *Educational Theory*, 47: 3.

Murphy, D. (1988) *Martin Buber's Philosophy of Education*. Irish Academic Press.

Riley, P. (1995) Supervision of Social Service Managers. In Pritchard, J. (Ed.) *Good Practice in Supervision: Statutory and Voluntary Organisations*. Jessica Kingsley.

Sawdon, C. and Sawdon, D. (1995) The Supervision Partnership: A Whole Greater than the Sum of its Parts. In Pritchard, J. (Ed.) *Good Practice in Supervision: Statutory and Voluntary Organisations*. Jessica Kingsley.

Stanners, C. (1995) Supervision in the Voluntary Sector. In Pritchard, J. (Ed.) *Good Practice in Supervision: Statutory and Voluntary Organisations*. Jessica Kingsley.

Vermes, P. (1988) *Buber*, Peter Halban.

Weinstein, J. (1975) *Buber and Humanistic Education*. Philosophical Library.

'. . . seeing is believing, but believing is seeing'[9]

Brian Belton

In this chapter I am going to look at what might be thought of as the very basic instruments that allow supervision to happen; the means by which we perceive events and how we mentally store the same. We often take our perceptions and recollections of 'reality' for granted. We might attend supervision and say 'this is what happened' with the intent of reviewing what happened, but is what we perceived or our memory of it actually what happened? If not, building the foundations of future practice on this picture might be a questionable venture.

Supervision is based on the reports (mostly verbal) of one person (the supervisee) to another (the supervisor). This interaction is, obviously, reliant on memory and its interaction with perception. For the most part, in everyday life, we do tend to believe what we see with our own eyes and we have a comparatively high level of faith in the account of eye witnesses to events, whether in terms of international news or routine events. However, the reliability of both memory and perception is suspect and certainly when our recall, together with our various senses, are called upon to work together, often the dependability of each seem to be more undermined by each other than producing something that might be understood as an accurate replay of events.

Trust in our senses has been leaking away for at least four centuries, no matter how much we add to them via lenses and rays. René Descartes argued that sense perception relies on the mind rather than on the body. For him we can know our mind better than we can know our body. He writes of a piece of wax which is observed in its solid form and its liquid form. After pointing out the difficulties of relying on the senses of the physical body to understand the nature of the wax he claims that perception is not a seeing or a touching; it isn't an imagining. It is, alone, an inspection on the part of the mind.

From this point Descartes reasons we can use our senses to help us understand the nature of things, but the senses alone are inadequate to determine truth (since they are often deceived or not up to the task). According to him, what can be known with certainty (truth) are those things we comprehend but this is restricted by way of our judgment, thinking, and understanding of them in our minds. Descartes' position does not of necessity reject the role of the senses in the process of understanding, but it does point out their limitations; what we see is not the truth but the truth as far as we can tell.

---

[9]Denis Waitley (*Empires of the Mind*).

In the modern era psychologists have known for some time that human memory is highly fallible; we make poor eye witnesses because we are unable to accurately remember what we see and hear. We unintentionally make up details to fill in the gaps to make sense of our past experience and emotions; fear, anxiety, sympathy have an effect on what we believe we see and hear. The recognition of finer features between ethnic groups is poor relative to the identification of subtle likenesses and differences within ethnic groups. If the suspect of a crime was wearing a red shirt at the time the crime was committed, any person wearing a red shirt in a subsequent identification parade, in the absence of anyone else in the parade wearing a red shirt, is likely to be identified as the suspect. We are very prone to such prompts. Mere likenesses seem to be easily transformed into definite and exact recognitions.

So we can't take eyewitness identification at face value and we can't straightforwardly take what has been claimed to have been seen as what in fact happened. Such considerations have a profound consequence on how we might understand what is happening in supervision and the character of what we might take to be reported facts (the material supervision is based on).

The trial of Adolf Beck

Adolf Beck, a middle aged man, who in the late 19th century was abiding in a shabby flat in Victoria Street, London, spent much of his later life deep in debt. However, deploying a blend of bogus assurances and his infinite charm, Beck had the ability to convince folk to give him cash. For instance, in 1884, although owing a massive amount of rent, he persuaded his landlord to loan him £1,600 (that would be something more than £100,000 today).

Beck had a history of losing copious amounts of money in business ventures and in 1895 he was skint. For all this, if you had seen him striding along the fashionable streets of London you wouldn't have guessed his potless state. He appeared to be well off Victorian gentleman, kitted out in a dapper coat with black silk lapels, carrying a silver topped umbrella.

One day, as Ottilei Meissonier came out of the Army and Navy Store, just yards from where Beck lived, she saw him and immediately said. 'Sir, I know you!' She recognised him to be the man who had conned her into giving him some gold rings and two watches. Following Ottilei's allegation, Beck made off, but his accuser followed him. On coming across a police officer Beck protested that Meissonier was harassing him, but his pursuer related that three weeks previously Beck had swindled her into handing over her valuables to him after he had stopped her on Victoria Street, claiming to be Lord Wilton, and asking if she was Lady Everton. Ottilei was in fact a modest music teacher. Following the subsequent chat Meissonier had invited him to come to her at home the following day.

The counterfeit Lord got to Ottilei's pad at the agreed time and asked, as she was both multilingual and musical, if he could escort her on a trip to the French Riviera with a few of his friends. Meissonier took up the offer. Following this he told her that her jewels were not of the quality needed for the trip and asked if he could trade them for some superior baubles, more suitable to the company she'd be keeping in la belle France. Ottilei was up for this and the phony aristocrat scribbled out a £40 cheque to cover the cost of the new wardrobe Meissonier would require for the Riviera. He left taking two rings and the two watches (straightforwardly lifting one of them).

The moment Lord Liar was out the door, Meissonier tore out to cash the cheque. But it turned out she had been passed a kite; the cheque was as spurious as its signatory, but to add insult to injury the branch of the bank it was drawn on did not exist.

Beck was hauled off to Rochester Road police station on the strength of Ottilei's accusation and it turned out that he fitted the description that Meissonier had provided the police with three weeks before. Another conned woman, Daisy Grant, along with Meissonier's servant, Mary Harvey, was asked to identify him. From an identification parade of seven men, only Beck had grey hair. Predictably, both Harvey and Grant chose him (the man they had seen weeks previously had also had a graying thatch). The police were more than satisfied with this result and Beck was charged and remanded in custody.

We now know that on live identification parades, which psychologists generally agree are flawed exercises, when the witness can see everyone at the same time, that they can make relative judgements about faces. This means they are liable to pick the best likeness out of a bunch of potentially not very close likenesses. So, even if none of the people are a particularly good or close likeness to the person being looked for, witnesses are likely to select someone who is the most like the person they saw commit the crime.

'I'd know him among a thousand.'

The sham peer who swindled women was of course a story that the newspapers of the time latched on to with gusto. The media hype about the debonair conman quickly produced a deluge of women who had been cheated in much the same manner as Meissonier. Nearly all of them identified Beck as the person who suckered them.

Kate Brakefield pointed to Beck in an eight-man line-up; 'I am satisfied he is the same man.' She proclaimed. Minnie Lewis picked Adolf out of a host of 14. She later let the court know, 'I had not had the least doubt in picking out the prisoner'. Juliette Kluth pointed out Beck from a throng of 18 men wandering around Westminster Police Yard. She was to testify later, 'I recognised the prisoner at once, as soon as I put my foot in the yard'. A year after she'd been had, in much the same fashion as the other women, Fanny Nutt was so confident that she was swindled by Beck that she declared in court, 'I'd know him among a thousand.'

At the conclusion of the investigation, Meissonier's first identification on Victoria Street was corroborated by no less than a dozen witnesses, one of whom was a police officer. The majority of these people had been absolutely certain Beck was the conman. He was charged with ten counts of theft and obtaining by false pretences. Beck had lacked a credible alibi for the dates concerned, but regardless of this it was thought totally unfeasible that every witness might be mistaken (for full evidence of the two Beck trials and the later commission of enquiry, see *The Trial of Adolf Beck* by Eric Watson, William Hodge, 1924).

The perpetrator of the scam had called himself 'Lord Wilton', 'Wilton de Willoughby' or slight variations on these titles. Immaculately dressed, all the women took note of his silver capped cane, weighty gold watch, top hat and overcoat with its silk lapels. The unfortunate dupes were also of a distinct social type. Almost invariably they lived on the margins of society as single women, working as music teachers, actresses or music-hall artistes; they had ambitions to move up the social pecking order but lacked the wherewithal to achieve such mobility. The swindler seemed to have built-in radar for such women.

These female victims often enhanced their earnings, as they diplomatically detailed in their statements, by 'seeing men for money'. They were, as such, vulnerable to a person who pledged a great deal, but they were used to conversing with people they didn't know and asking them to visit them if they thought it might be financially worthwhile.

In the guise of Lord Wilton the man told his victims that he was rich and let them know about his estate in Lincolnshire, its ten gardeners, his property around the Brompton Road and his impressive annual income from the same. Usually he talked about being on the lookout for a housekeeper, which at that time would have been understood as code for a paid 'live-in mistress' – a sort of respectable prostitute. The women were guaranteed riding lessons, travel abroad and parties. All this promised to be a very attractive package for women of their station.

Having established his remarkable credentials, his Lordship would inform his host that her jewellery and general attire would need upgrading and ask for rings so he could make sure the new ones he was going to buy for them would fit. Likewise he took watches, saying he would replace them with better time pieces. He would write a cheque for a bank with a high status address in St James', telling his victims to anticipate a visit from a commissionaire from the Carlton Club in around an hour, delivering their valuables and newly purchased jewellery. After this he left, occasionally (and somewhat outrageously) asking for change to cover his cab fare.

This performance is significant as it had a history. A trial in 1877 judged a trickster, known as John Smith, using the same nom de plume 'Lord Willoughby', conning females, using a near duplicate tale. But if the so called Lord Willoughby and Lord Wilton were the same individual, Adolf Beck could not be the culprit, as in 1877 Beck was in Peru unsuccessfully trying to establish a theatre project.

During March 1896, Beck's barrister at his trail tried to introduce evidence of the previous conviction of Smith. He had little ammunition other than this. Sir Forrest Fulton, the second most senior judge at the Old Bailey, who as a youthful barrister had unbelievably prosecuted the trail of 1877, denied the admission of such material as it '. . . related to another and distinct issue, and one calculated to mislead the jury'. The conned women provided their evidence and while Beck consistently protested his innocence, he was convicted and, at the age of 55, given seven years hard labour.

From prison Beck undertook a fraught campaign of letter-writing, pleading with the authorities to revisit his case. But it was to no avail. He had served two years when John Smith's former prison governor reviewed the latter's file to find that Smith was

Jewish and as such circumcised. With no explanation Beck was given an examination which provided irrefutable verification that, if the same man had committed the crimes, Beck was not the perpetrator. Sir Forrest Fulton, Beck's trail judge, was given this information by the Home Office; however no action was taken to review Beck's case.

In 1901 Beck was released from prison, returning to his former indigent life style. A couple of years later the same scam was going on again. A well turned-out gentleman, again a Lord Willoughby, was conning women. In 1904 Pauline Scott rocked up at Scotland Yard saying that she had been cheated out of a watch and a ring by his Lordship, who she had met in Oxford Street. The police set an ambush, thinking they knew who the man was. Just like the 1895 Meissonier identification, Scott, escorted by a detective constable, challenged Beck in the street. 'You are the man who took my jewellery and sovereign,' she accused. Once again Beck refuted the allegation. 'No, I am not. I do not know you. I have never seen you in my life before.' But Adolf was arrested, charged, tried and convicted after witnesses adamantly testified that he had swindled them.

Days after Beck's second conviction, on 7 July 1904, while he was banged up in Brixton prison, an elderly, extravagantly dressed gentleman, convinced a couple of sisters to hand over several rings and half-a-crown, after making extraordinary promises. He claimed to be Lord Willoughby. But the sisters had their doubts and as he made his exit, they persuaded their landlord to follow this person. Initially the would-be aristocrat went to a jeweller for a valuation of his ill-gotten gains. From there he made his way to a pawnbroker. The man was arrested upon the summons of a police officer; he was the John Smith, circa 1877, aka Frederick Meyer. Fred had been out of the London loop for a number of years, profitably plying his trade in the USA.

Meyer's arrest in 1904 motivated more women to come forward to make charges about his activities. The fact of his circumcision, provided by his former prison governor to the Home Office, was picked up by the newspapers. Subsequently the press went ballistic about how such a wrong could have been allowed to occur; why was the intactness of Beck's foreskin not made more of? Beck was set free within days and subsequently pardoned of both convictions. He was offered £2,000 compensation at first but at the insistence of the media he eventually got £5,000 (roughly equivalent to £350,000 today). The Master of the Rolls, second most senior judge in the Realm, led a government inquiry. No one in authority came out of that well, certainly not the Home Office or the 1896 trail judge Sir Forrest Fulton.

In the light of the committee of inquiry's conclusions a year later, the Court of Appeal was established with the purpose of reviewing the safety of criminal convictions and to rectify possible miscarriages of justice.

More than a passing glance

The Importance of Beck's case is not to show up official torpor and ineptitude, nor the insensitive inanity of the courts, such things are historically well known and catalogued. Becks' trails demonstrate that 16 individuals (including police officers) autonomously, in identity parades recognised Beck as the criminal. The misdemeanors perpetrated by

Meyer (aka Smith, aka Lord Willoughby) were not swift 'hit and run' heists; the wronged got much more than a passing glance at the felon in a badly lit back alley. The witnesses were in conversation with 'Lord Sham' for up to an hour, mostly in a convivial context with good light. They had every advantage in terms of correctly identifying the swindler but they, without fail, blew it.

This case alone can't suffice to question the practice of supervision as a means of reviewing experience. However, it is just one of very many examples that demonstrate how our memory, in tandem with conditions, psychological disposition and our eminently fallible sensory apparatus, makes for unreliable impressions. Sometimes people providing the fullest description of a person will be the least likely to identify them. Recall and recognition, although both involving memory, are two dissimilar cognitive processes. Recall involves bringing the memory one has, for example, of a face, into the mind's eye. One does that in order to describe this face to another person or other people. Recognition involves comparing one face with another face that one sees in front of them with one's memory of a face, and asking if this face is the same face that one has a memory of. Bringing recall and recognition together rather than being mutually supportive capacities, can result in a totally corrupted perspective.

At the same time, humans are not that great at remembering facets of identity. Some time ago I carried out what is a fairly common experiment with a male colleague. He asked random strangers in the street for directions. When the person seeking directions was out of sight I asked the person who gave the directions to describe the individual asking for directions. So, this 32-year-old man with Scottish accent, who was six feet tall, had blue eyes and black hair was variously described as being in his mid-20s to 45, having, brown or green eyes, being anywhere from five feet eight inches to six feet two inches tall, and of foreign, eastern European, or Irish origin. His hair was described as ginger and brownish, although some people gave him a hat. Most responses were fairly definite. No description was entirely accurate; few got more than two elements of my colleague's description correct. This is pretty much standard for this experiment, but maybe try it for yourself.

What one individual pictures as a 28-year-old is often quite different to what another person might assess. What constitutes a 'big nose'? People are colour blind in diverse ways, and as many as one in ten of us do not know we carry a particular 'colour blind gene'. So what one person might see as a 'green cardigan' another might take to be a 'brown jumper'; one person's blue eyes will be green (the character of the light will also make a difference to such distinctions). Some individuals have better eye sight than others etc. Added to this we do not store faces in our memory as a collection of features; we seem to represent the whole face. At the same time there are differences in the way we remember features. For instance, hair appears to be the most salient feature for Caucasians; for this group changing hair tends to change the way the whole face looks. The colour of skin can be difficult to describe for most people; it is hard to get an agreement on what the difference is between 'swarthy', 'East European', 'dark', 'tanned', 'Mediterranean', 'North African' and 'Asian'. People also disagree what being black, mixed heritage or white, African or West Indian might be. I recall a group of people arguing if an particular entertainer was 'Arabic', 'Jewish', 'Italian', 'Spanish' , 'Welsh' or 'Gypsy'; she was actually Iranian.

Added to this, it is not uncommon for people to claim to recognise total strangers when asked to do this from a selection of pictures, particularly if a picture is of someone smiling. The effect is further influenced if the picture being looked at by someone known to the subject in the picture; when we view such pictures we tend to get the feeling that the person in the picture knows us.

Laslo Virag

Misidentification was one of the main reasons for establishing the English Court of Criminal Appeal in 1907, but it wasn't until the 1970s that the criminal justice system fully recognised the fallibility of eyewitness testimony. In 1974 Laslo Virag walked free from prison with a Royal Pardon. He had been sentenced to 10 years because eight eyewitnesses had positively identified him as an armed robber who had shot and injured a police officer. Such was the credibility of eye witness testimony that no other evidence was put forward by the prosecution.

Identification by eye witnesses has, by such cases, been proved to be fragile and as such needs to be treated with great caution. Nevertheless it is convincing to have someone who was present at an incident or event who seems able to recreate the emotion and the sequence of events, but this is nearly always, in the first instance, seductive and as such misleading.

Human beings tend to be not very good at describing strangers. We find it hard to imagine a specific face, or it is difficult to draw a face from our memory into our mind's eye. Even when we manage this, we find it very tough to describe that face. We do not appear to have the language to describe what an individual aspect of appearance looks like in much detail. This is not surprising; words are words and looks are not words. Human language, as we know it, is a relatively recent phenomenon; it emerged around 10,000 years ago out of a human history of over 200,000 years. The evolution of our perceptive equipment is of course vastly older. It does not simplistically guide our language, just as an amplifier does not develop a musical score.

As such, we need to be aware of the dangers of hanging on the every word of an eye witness; the brain is not a camera. We tend to see what we want to see and everybody sees a situation at least a bit differently; on many occasions one person appears to see something in a completely different way from another or others. The vast majority of events brought to supervision involve people; in fact these occurrences are defined by the perceived actions of particular human beings. However, when I describe people and their actions to you in supervision, that situation is not what happened; it is a memory of my experience mediated by my senses. At the same time, how you might picture what I have described in your head is going to be different to how I view events and people in my mind. This means that not only am I not thinking of what actually happened, you are not thinking even what I'm thinking; what you are thinking of is a sort of third event that is at best only tangentially connected to the event that actually happened.

Seeing is believing

Eye witnesses have been responsible for sending a huge number of innocent people to prison. In 1970s there were so many that the Law Lord Patrick Devlin in his report of 1976 concluded that eye witness evidence alone should not be enough to convict. But this did not mean that it was only the system that may have been at fault. The fundamental problem with eye witness testimony is that people fail to recall exactly what happened.

Neither the brain nor the mind have a place for an unflawed memory of happenings, nor do they record accurately what we hear or see in the order that it happened. The process of putting together the impressions that we use to recreate events in our mind is done largely outside of our consciousness. This includes memories of what happened, but what we are putting together is not the event, it is a reconstruction, and what we finish up with might be at least partly, perhaps wholly, a false picture, as it will include the input from other aspects of mind, like imagination. Part of the fallibility of human memory is that it is easy to include something based on the unconscious assumption that it is part of a memory when it isn't. You will be able to understand the questions this raises about what one might bring to supervision and also how it is heard, understood and eventually recorded (from memory) by the supervisor.

Most of us when we think about human memory conjure up a sort of video analogy in our heads. In part, this is because visual images come to mind when we recollect past events. However, there is nothing one is able to directly identify in the brain that demonstrates that there are particular sets of neurons firing in a certain place or places within the neocortex that might produce a flawless record of the breakfast you had with your partner or children this morning. A memory is the culmination of lots of parts or aspects of the brain. Virtual networks are created and out of these emerge the mental impression that is one's experience of the memory. Within that construction process there are infinite opportunities for mistakes; all memory is fragmentary; memory (m) is time (t) condensed (c); ($m = tc$). So passages will be forgotten, creating amnesic elements. This being the case, memory (compacted time) is simultaneously inaccurate and correct, but overall it is nothing more than impression produced by the interplay of reality, imagination, the impact of the unconscious (that includes influences from our background/experience). The limits of our perceptive equipment and how we might want to see ourselves and portray our behaviour to others.

For all this, we do trust our own eyes. Perhaps more than anything else in life we believe what we see. However what one sincerely believes and remembers one has seen and what has actually occurred might (and often are) two completely different things. When we deal with floods of information we are only going to take so much in before our brains filter this material. We tend to remember what we are interested in and reject much of the rest, even though some of this might be relevant or even critical to understanding a situation. The brain holds on to what it takes to be pertinent information and when we are uncertain about details (the gaps that have been left by our filtering) we often inadvertently make them up (fill in the gaps) or in effect, guess.

This is slotting our ideas about what should have happened (logically to us) into an incomplete memory about what really did happen. We, at the same time, associate things with what was actually there and these associations are encompassed into memories about other incidents or situations; 'It was raining so the man had a hat on'; 'My aunt Maud is a redhead and she wears a bangle on her left hand, so this other redheaded, middle-aged woman also had a bangle on her left hand'. Actually, memories are inventions that can produce a scenario that never happened in reality. But once we bring this construction into being its authenticity is confirmed with every telling. What occurred is just a seed of what we end up relating as reality.

Now, so far I've just been writing about relatively simple identity choices, involving the identification of just a single individual. Imagine what happens when we put our memory and perceptive equipment to work to produce an image of what happened to a whole group of people in a complex, interactive situation, relating to personal histories, attitudes and personalities, the sort of material commonly brought to supervision.

Scripts

From a very early age we develop scripts in memory. We do this primary because we dislike the unknown. This is probably understandable if thought of in terms of survival mechanisms. If you are going to a new place or meeting someone for the first time, you can feel a bit unsure, that is a low level experience of a characteristic fear of the unknown. As we all fear the unknown, from the age of around three we begin to develop rules and regulations about life; what normally happens in a cinema or a hospital for example; human beings develop scripts about life situations out of their imagination, recall, general and particular experiences. These scripts impinge on everything we relate about the world, to ourselves and others. Thus our experience, perhaps as much as immediate actuality, shapes what we say we see and hear and our oration of how something was.

If you are an experienced supervisor you can see these scripts reoccurring. People take on a characteristic way of telling their stories about what happened to them. The longest supervisory relationships I have had were for nine and ten years. From my recordings I found that each of these people had a repertoire of about nine scenarios that were repeated almost in a loop. Permutations of the scenarios intermingled at times, but in the main they stayed pretty much on track. This is a situation I have experienced repeatedly and have talked to other supervisors about. Our scripts might sometimes be like a powerful route map for us; they explain the apparently inexplicable and give us the comfort and security of the impression that most things are predictable. But scripts are not reality, just as the road-scape on satnav is not the streets, roads and lanes that stretch out before me, and the narrative I relate in supervision is not what happened in actuality.

The world-making mind

Our mind makes up the world for us. We witness an assault and can create a weapon that wasn't there (as it explains what happened in the absence of any other explanation

– the person attacked was bleeding). We add and subtract inferences that make what happened make more sense for us and we implicate our own personal scripts into this. But this doesn't mean it will make sense for everyone because we make sense of the world in highly individual ways. We have personal interpretations of reality; my judgement about distance, time, people's ages will often differ from even those closest to me. I can look across a river and say the other bank is 15 meters away; my son will tell me it is 50 meters. Part of this might be about me being brought up on imperial measurements and him having used metric all his life. But relative awareness and eyesight might also be amongst the many factors influencing our particular judgements. People invariably disagree when making estimates about the size of a room that is new to them. Try it in terms of age. When you are next with a person you know well, a spouse or friend, pick three strangers out in a café or waiting area and individually guess their ages. You will probably find a level of disagreement. The impact of experience, the relative capacity of our senses, and what we want to see, will all have an impact.

Memory as accident

Memory might be understood as the accidental outcome of what one hears or sees as it is not something we actually control. Even consciously attempting to recall something, for example a series of events or putting a face to a name, does not automatically mean that one will remember what one has tried to commit to memory. At the same time we do forget things or 'misremember', sometimes ultimately recollecting occurrences, situations and statements that did not actually take place as we remember them; occasionally what we recall has little or no relation to what in fact took place. Many of you reading this will recognise such situations. Mostly, this has little if any impact on our lives, but if I am relating to an intimate client situation, if I am looking to formulate a critical intervention that will impact on their quality of life, happiness or well-being, it can have expansive, exponential and potentially devastating consequences.

In the realm of memory there is also a sphere that exists between accident and intention that is created by the intervention of the unconscious. This is the locale where what Goffman (1959) called 'front' might be understood to emanate from. We have a tendency to portray events as we want people to see them, but we have an innate propensity to protect our personal integrity. This line of defence might be understood as part of the survival instinct. As such, we have a penchant for portraying ourselves in a way that we want people to perceive us, and (awkwardly, at same time) the way we believe they want to see us. Even when I am critical of my own actions, say as part of a critical review in supervision, I am demonstrating my professional veracity so enhancing my profile; my get-out clause in this is 'I made mistake, but I am showing how good I am by being ready to address it'. So whatever I am relating to becomes a tale of redemption or a confessional process. For this I expect the consolation of absolution: a big fat red tick! But even with regard to the most mundane situations we are likely to have our own view that in some way or another will underwrite or justify our actions.

For example, some time ago I and my family were visiting my sister-in-law, Adelle, in York and we were looking for somewhere entertaining and edifying to take our young son. Adelle suggested the 'Grimsby Fishing Heritage Centre', and proceeded to act out its many exciting attractions, which included the experience of an astonishing replication of the pitch and yaw of a fishing vessel on the high seas. Feet wide apart, in her kitchen, Adelle swayed and staggered, and we were there, not just at the Heritage Centre, but hunting the bright shoals of herrings on the great Atlantic swells. The next day we made for the Heritage Centre, our mental appetites whetted with the expectation of adventure! Now, while the Grimsby Fishing Heritage Centre is not unimpressive within its own terms, to say that as a family we were underwhelmed by our collective experience of it would be about accurate. The mechanical deck, a sort of gentle, four-way see-saw, notwithstanding.

What was going on here? You might take Adelle to have been straightforwardly lying, but this doesn't make much sense as she was advocating we should experience the Heritage Centre for ourselves; she was not simply 'bigging up' her own experience. She certainly wanted us to have a good time having travelled up from London to York, so care was a factor. However, front probably played a part as she was showing herself to have spent her time in an interesting and exciting way and to be a person informed about good experiences in her vicinity. There is also potential biographical pollution; Adelle was born and brought up in an exciting place at an exhilarating time (London in the 1960s). When she married and moved to York some of her friends and family found it puzzling that she would want to leave the lively metropolis for a relative provincial backwater (this is not 'fact' it is relative perception). While she was not a person to spend time justifying her actions, there was always something in the background saying 'this place has its attractions too!' So, Adelle's wants and our wants, the way we expressed our wants and the way she related her wants, shaped the story of the Heritage Centre. This kind of interplay, pollution and justification will play a part in supervision, both on the part of the supervisor and the supervisee; to deny this is to fool oneself.

Three stage memory

That supervision is propped up by the unreliable set of tools that memory is demands our consideration, understanding and in the last analysis, management, but the other pillar of supervision is the fragile function of mind that is memory.

It is pretty common knowledge that by most tests of human memory are only about 60 per cent reliable, but in order to grasp how our memory can be misleading it is crucial to be aware there are three-stages in memory operation. The initial stage is encoding, this is the means of processing of the physical sensory information coming into the brain. If we are going to remember something we need to be concentrating on it to some extent. For most of us, the usual street atmosphere is a bustling, chaotic situation; a vast stream of data taken in by our senses that the brain is called upon to manage. This information or stimulation is mediated via what we hear, smell, feel and see; it is organised, sifted and filtered by the processes of mind.

At the same time, the human perceptive equipment, and thus our minds, are affected by what we anticipate perceiving. Although the mind and our perceptive tools are not really separate entities, this process can be thought of as a two-way street, perception hitting on mind, mind mediating perception. This happens because otherwise we would be unable decode what we perceive – there is literally too much going on.

As such, a couple of people might witness precisely the same event but each could (and probably will) decipher it in an entirely different manner. A particular witness may see someone as intimidating and so provide embellished interpretation of that individual's menacing demeanor, body shape or size, while another witness could perceive and decipher the same person as just another bystander with perhaps a rather awkward manner.

Storage is the second stage of memory. Our memory is not a sort of elaborate filing cabinet from which we can conveniently whip-out a recollection. Even uncomplicated memories are very complex structures, which are stored in bits and pieces right across and throughout the topography of the brain. This means that the last stage of memory, retrieval, is something of a chancy matter.

Typically retrieval operates via prompts, like a place, a person's look, or a period in our life. Say you bring to mind a journey you've made; you will immediately begin recalling aspects of that trip. However, these elements will evoke other memories of similar journeys, but also similar people, places, situations and incidents, like those you recall being involved with in the memories of the journey you started with. All these considerations affect and infect the memory of your journey and all journeys like this journey.

Retrieval cues work because they replicate the circumstances at the point when you encoded memories. Although we sort of think we are actually or literally rebuilding the context, we are not. What we are doing is making an image in our head about what happened, but we can't help but include other recollections and interpretations. The result is, with the help of the imagination and other factors of mind, a belief about what happened, but that is certainly not what happened. As might be expected, this erosion and addition process tends to become more profound the more time there is between the event and the relating of the same.

So when I walk into my once fortnightly supervision session and start talking about something that happened ten days ago, I am telling a story about what happened, but also what might have happened and what my mind tells me should have happened (and should not have happened). This narrative will be shaped by my own biography, bias, imagination, hopes, fears, desires and feelings. In short it will be a patchwork of thoughts, shaped by my limited perceptions and a range of recollections and as such will not be *the* event I am recounting but *an* event in itself: the story is more about me than anything else.

Unreliable reflection

According to Munro (2011a: 87, 6.11):

> *Experience on its own, however, is not enough. It needs to be allied to reflection – time and attention given to mulling over the experience and learning from it. This is*

often best achieved in conversation with others, in supervision, for example, or in discussions with colleagues.

Munro goes on to call on Oakeshott (1989: 33) to lament:

. . . the limitations of a 'crowded' life where people are continually occupied and engaged but have no time to stand back and think.

Ibid.

This is hard to argue with, however for Munro (2011a: 90, 6.25) it becomes clear that reflection alone is not enough:

Supervision and case consultations . . . are critical in helping practitioners draw out their reasoning so that it can be reviewed.

She goes on to state, relating to Gigerenzer (2002: 228):

Gut feelings are neither stupid nor perfect. They take advantage of the evolved capacities of the brain and are based on rules of thumb that enable us to act fast and with astounding accuracy, shown, for example, in our ability to recognise faces.

But, supported by Gilovich, Griffin and Kahneman, D. (2008: 91, 6.26):

They are not infallible, as research shows, because intuitive judgments are vulnerable to predictable types of error. Critical challenge by others is needed to help social workers catch such biases and correct them – hence the importance of supervision.

Here is a clear indication that supervision, to be fit for purpose, needs the supervisor to be active as a critic and sensitive to the frailty of reflection. This, of course, provides a model of developing professional judgement; questioning the taken and assessing the possibility of alternatives.

The credo of 'reflective practice' does suffer from critical examination. It sometimes seems that within the canon of supervision 'reflection', which is constantly premised as being central to the point and process of the exercise, is taken as almost infallible. The primary focus of this reflection is our experience and the evidencing of our practice (this is what I did, this is how I did it, this is why I did it). However mistracing memory can cause dramatic errors that emphasise how unreliable identification evidence is, but the same is true for the process of reflection, the very activity that much of the literature on supervision sees as the 'royal road' to practice development and professional enlightenment. The more we reflect, because of all the mistraces that are bound to be provoked, the further we get from the reality of what happened. This is a sort of internal Chinese whispers effect.

For example, a witness to an assault outside a nightclub was requested to indicate to the court the perpetrator of the attack. The witness pointed out the victim who sat in the public gallery. The surprised judge asked the witness to confirm the identification and once more the witness pointed at the victim. The technical title for this is a 'source attribution error'. The witness had recalled two intimately connected roles from the same memory and had confused the assailant with the victim. This was a result of reflection on the situation.

An infamous incidence of this is the case of Don Thompson, an Australian barrister and an authority on identification. Thompson made his way into a police station to visit a client he was representing. The police officer at the station reception almost immediately arrested him, taking him to be a rapist. For the officer, Thompson's face matched an e-fit (a computer aided form of identikit) of this criminal. The unsuspecting barrister was of course totally shocked. An identity parade was organised and the victim, the person who of course had the biggest hand in the production of the e-fit, identified Thompson as the rapist. Providentially, the barrister had a solid alibi; Thompson had been in the company of the commissioner of police and the local mayor at the time of the rape. In fact they had all appeared on a live television programme together; ironically they were debating miscarriages of justice and identification. At the time of the rape the victim had been watching Thompson on television; her mind had somehow switched the rapist's face with his. But what is important in terms of supervision is that the process of the police officer identification and the subsequent identity parade were the obvious elements in ongoing reflective activity that must have involved questions like:

- Who is this person?
- Is this person the rapist?
- What does this person look like?
- What does the rapist look like?
- Are you sure this is the rapist?
- Why are you sure this is the rapist?

In short, this replicates the kind of interrogation a supervisor might make of a supervisee's convictions about their practice or an event related about their work.

The woman was absolutely sure she had picked the right person and as such her witness statement was probably convincing. But what if Thompson had not have been a barrister and/or had lacked such a cast iron alibi? Identification is often unchallenge-able; therefore it is both powerful and so dangerous. A misidentified defendant might be left with just their own denial to defend themselves with. Around 75 per cent of the people on Death Row who, via DNA evidence, have been proved by the 'Innocence Project' in the United States to have been wrongfully convicted, were convicted through identification by eyewitnesses.

Reflection as introspection

The paradigm of 'reflective practice' might be understood as a harnessing of introspection. For Wilson (2002) introspection can lead people to ignore intuitions and feelings that are difficult to put into words, but which might be quite important. The danger of introspection is that we can talk ourselves into feelings that we don't really have. According to Wilson and Schooler (1991) introspection causes people:

> *... to make choices that, compared with control subjects', corresponded less with expert opinion. Analysing reasons can focus people's attention on nonoptimal criteria, causing them to base their subsequent choices on these criteria. Evaluating multiple attributes can moderate people's judgments, causing them to discriminate less between the different alternatives.*

For Bechtel and Graham (1999):

> *... introspection is an unreliable instrument, so much evidence on which our own mental analysis is based is derived from faulty instruments. Introspection does not even have the appearance of reality ... so we avoid the self-deception that introspection entails.*

Contamination

Spend a minute viewing an abstract painting, ideally one that is new to you. Maybe ask three or four others to share this task with you. Try to say what the picture brings to mind, or what it reminds you of; a dog, a car, a doughnut? After two or three weeks, from memory, have a go at painting the picture yourself from memory, perhaps together with the other people who you asked to look at the original painting. The likeness does not have to be great; this is just about getting to something that resembles the original painting. You can use crayons or coloured pencils if paint is not practical. Take no more than five or six minutes to complete the task.

Typically humans tend to remember what something reminds them of rather than the thing itself. If you complete the above task with others you might include a colour choice that was not in the original picture; because that choice of colour is available most people will include it. This is a kind of contamination of memory.

Contamination can be crucial in terms of our practice. Often people introduce unintended and purposeful contamination to our memories to claim something happened in the way it did or didn't happen. Again this is something you can try for yourself. Ask someone about an event or situation. They may talk about a person and not mention their size. Asking 'what size was he?' is different to asking 'was he big? or 'how big was he?'. 'He sounds like a big bloke' has yet more impact. All or any of these interjections might provoke agreement that he was big, or an over emphasis on how he lacked bigness, and thus is said to be 'small'. Size was not a factor previously but the contaminating question highlighted it. This seems fairly innocuous, but imagine a conversation between an adult and small child about an accusation of abuse allegedly connected to witchcraft, something that was a source of moral panic a few years ago:

Adult: Did a man come into the room?
Child: Which man?
Adult: The witch man?
Child: The witch man?

The adult has heard:

Adult: Did a man come into the room?
Child: Witch man!
Adult: The witch man?
Child: The witch man

The conversation continues with contamination interacting with imagination and the filling of gaps on the part of both parties:

Adult: And what did the witch man do?
Child: He cast a spell
Adult: What was the spell?
Child: He turned me into a cat
Adult: Why did the witch man do that?
Child: He likes stroking cats

Human memory is dominated by one's understanding of an experience. If I understand an experience in a certain way, for example, for me an abstract painting resembles a doughnut, and I have a go at reproducing it some time later, my picture will reflect the doughnut label that I have given it. If a witch or a cat is introduced into my recollections I may find a space for them as I turn recall into a collaborative fiction/story. The source of the knowledge in my memory comes from what I imagine, think, understand and fantasise about more so than from a picture postcard of reality. In many cases people cannot make that discrimination. They take that which their mind has labelled and their memory has reproduced as reality.

However, it is not unusual for the nature of reality to be contested. Take the saga of The Millennium Bridge, officially known as the London Millennium Footbridge, a steel suspension bridge for pedestrians crossing the Thames, linking Bankside with the City (located between Southwark and Blackfriars Railway Bridge). Construction of the bridge began in 1998, and it was opened on 10 June 2000. Londoners soon nicknamed the crossing the 'Wobbly Bridge' as it had a tendency to sway, move or vibrate (there was no real agreement about exactly what it was doing) slightly when it was being relatively well used. This movement was hardly perceptible to some, experienced as 'fun' by others, while a number of people found it uncomfortable and disconcerting. How the bridge was experienced differed according to conditions, the disposition and number of people using it. Soon the story of what the bridge 'was' or had the potential to 'be' became established.

The bridge was eventually closed for almost two years while expensive modifications were made to eliminate the wobble. It was reopened in 2002, wobble-less. However, there are some who believe that it continues to move, while others mourn its lack of movement and individuals from both sides of this perception avoid or even refuse to use it because of these perceptions: it continues to be known as the 'wobbly bridge'.

This is just one example, and one could come up with many more, both public and private, that shows the nature of reality to be tenuous. As reality becomes more complicated, populated with different perceptions, understandings, interpretations, of relationships, unexpressed intentions, mistakes and instinctive behaviour it becomes less and less tangible. This is the stuff of supervision.

Supervisors can also miss or misinterpret crucial factors. Notions about what one might want from a supervisee or what one might want them to end up with, incline supervisors to ask questions that will invite the wanted answers. These are often called leading questions. When a supervisee is talking to a supervisor about their experience of a situation or an event it is important to keep in mind that this is a memory, not actuality. As we have seen, memory is constructed and fragmentary, at all times it is subjected to unconscious inferences made by both the person memorising and the person they are relating their memory to. It is arguable if it is possible to avoid projecting our experience and culture onto others. For instance, if we see behaviour as unacceptable we will associate the person who carries out that behaviour as suspect. We can (and people do) deny this, but our principles and values are hardly ever suspended. For all our proclamations about being 'neutral', 'objective' or 'non-judgemental', human beings are driven by emotions, feelings and the associations these are created by impulses as unconscious as blinking; even a corpse fails to be entirely neutral.

This apart, supervision is about more than achieving accurate memories. Often there are other requirements and agenda that are being considered, so the interference of the unconscious is added to by conscious mediations of reality; 'I want my supervisor to feel I am an effective practitioner', 'I want my supervisee to feel they are learning from our work together' are perhaps the most benign wants that can distort almost everything that goes on in supervision.

Even if we manage not to verbalise our feelings or judgements, facial expression and body language can unconsciously give our attitudes and response away. One study at UCLA indicated that as much as 93 per cent of communication effectiveness is determined by non-verbal cues. Another study suggested that the impact of a performance was determined 7 per cent by the words used, 38 per cent by voice quality, and 55 per cent by the nonverbal communication. So even when we think we are 'in control' of ourselves we are not in control, it is just a story about our own self control that we have adopted or been convinced of.

Unreliable reliability

The Law Lord's report of the 1970s had it that trials founded merely on identification evidence should be allowed only in exceptional circumstances and, if there are no exceptional conditions, the trial should be halted. It was recommended that identification cases should be restricted as it was thought to be impossible to evaluate the accuracy of an alleged identification. They also saw that a code of practice governing the way identification procedures are conducted was desirable. However, this was disregarded by the government of the day. Ministers of State rarely agree measures that threaten to bring down the number of convictions.

Ultimately, the Court of Appeal reconciled the situation by way of the Turnbull case. This set out guiding principles as to how identification evidence should be approached and used if a defendant contests identification. These guidelines are passed to a jury by way of a judicial direction:

I must therefore warn you of the special need for caution before convicting the defendant in reliance on the evidence of identification. A witness who is convinced in his own mind may as a result be a convincing witness, but may nevertheless be mistaken. Mistakes can also be made in the recognition of someone known to a witness, even of a close friend or relative. You should therefore examine carefully the circumstances in which the identification was made, or how long did he have the person he says was the defendant under observation? At what distance? In what light? Did anything interfere with the observation? Had the witness ever seen the person he observed before? If so, how often? If only occasionally, had he any special reason for remembering him? How long was it between the original observation and the identification to the police? Is there any marked difference between the description given by the witness to the police when he was first seen by them, and the appearance of the defendant?

These guidelines represent a typical illustration of the way in which common law, by way of a judge's direction to the jury, works to secure the evidence; to ensure it is 'fair'. This is the way the law gets the best of both worlds. The jury has access to evidence by way of identification, providing the judge has cautioned them about its hazards. Unfortunately there is no such caution set within the supervision process, which is based, in effect, on the eye witness statements of the supervisee (and sometimes the eye witness statements of others that the supervisee relates to the supervisor). For the most part (understandably) the supervisor pretty much just believes what they are told by the supervisee, and what is described is taken to be fact (probably because there is little other alternative within the limitations of the process); a given event or situation is taken to have been more or less flawlessly reconstructed when what has been portrayed is likely to be anything but this.

For all this, it is questionable just how effective these guidelines are in terms of the avoidance of erroneous identifications which can convict the wrong individual. If one applies the Turnbull guidelines to the case of Adolf Beck, having taken in that direction, what jury would be likely to acquit poor old Beck? The women involved had extended time with Meyer, in good conditions in terms of observation (ample light, no obstacles to vision) far superior to many identification cases. Meissonier picked him out in the street. Beck was similar in appearance to Meyer, matching the crucial initial description (when memories were relatively fresh) provided to police by witnesses. The quality of the identification was about as good as possible. The women, being certain, having made up their minds, were totally persuasive. According to one, Fanny Nutt, she would '. . . know him among a thousand.' Given that weight of evidence where was the room for doubt for any jury?

There were some discrepancies that Beck's defence barrister missed. Several of the witnesses when giving their initial description (Meissonier was one of these) recalled a minor scar on the swindler's jaw line, Beck had no such mark. The first descriptions of a few of the witnesses described the con artist as significantly stouter than Beck. In some cases there was a long period of time between a witness first seeing the criminal and identifying Beck. However, even if the defence had picked up on these issues, without exception the witnesses picked Beck out. How could the accuracy of identification be reasonably questioned given the level of corroboration?

It has been estimated that between six and seven per cent of witnesses who positively identify a felon are mistaken. Not a huge figure you might say, however that number grows as each witness attends an identification parade. Amongst five witnesses, one making a false positive identification is between 30 and 35 per cent likely and the risk of being wrong grows with each additional witness. If there are nine witnesses attending an identification parade the arithmetic has it that one of them will identify the suspect as the person who committed the crime, regardless if the criminal is in the line up or not.

As it is an occupational hazard for a supervisor to mistakenly (or otherwise) influence interpretations made by a supervisee (it is arguable that by just being in the same room as a supervisee a supervisor does this) it is simple for any questioner to unintentionally influence the result of identification. If we are to be scientific a 'double blind' aspect is required. That would mean that in the process of identification both subject and the tester would be ignorant of the 'right' choice. This of course can never be the case in supervision, firstly as we insist on dealing with what we call 'relationships' (implying an intimate knowledge of the 'other') but also we are reliant on the supervisee to bring their choices, accusations, assumptions, biases, mistakes etc. with them to the situation to be presented as the 'facts' of practice to work (or perhaps more realistically, build on) via the distorting process of reflection.

Context retrieval

Context retrieval techniques can draw out recollections that may otherwise have been forgotten or missed out. Cognitive interviews, frequently undertaken by police when questioning child witnesses, attempt to restore in the child's mind the specific context of the time and incident they are trying to recall. The witness is asked to talk about the entire day. As you can imagine, this is a very long-winded process, something that would not necessarily fit well into a supervision regime but also immaterial recollections can prompt more important or relevant memories.

Dredging the memory can also trigger latent 'memory traces'; a string of connections over a network of neurons. These are bits of memory disseminated all over and throughout the brain. Memory trawls are fairly arbitrary and there is always the threat that any memory trace activated could cause misattribution, or a mistrace. For example, you are talking to someone you know and you remember a theatre production you both attended. However, this person says you actually did not attend that play together; it was another production you both saw. You give this some thought and recognise they are correct. You had confused two different memories because they had similar aspects (theatre, yourself, this person). People do this sort of thing all the time and sometimes there is no way, time or will to verify if one has or has not made the mistake.

Supervisors are often advised to make notes about supervision as soon as possible after a session, just as youth workers taking supervision are counselled to make their practice recordings as close in time to events recorded as they can. Time does make a difference to our recall, but it is by no means certain that the sooner we record what we have seen that the recording will be more accurate. Swift recording seems to do little more than offer the chance of lowering inaccuracies. But as soon as you start writing your total memory (encompassing all like situations and associated people) will start to interact with your imagination. As I write 'It was like this' I will begin an unconscious trawl of my experience, which includes fantasy, expectation and mistraces, and this will potentially be added to the pot in what is a pretty random way. So, what was 'like this' will include a proportion of everything that was 'like this' for me. Writing about an event is also a third hand description; it follows on from:

- the event
- my perception of the event
- my presentation of the event

When these recordings are used as a prompt to my relating the event to my supervisor, that relating is a forth hand version of the event. The event forming in the supervisor's mind is a fifth adaptation and whatever they record in their notes is the sixth incarnation. It is not unusual (indeed it might be considered good practice) for supervisors to take supervision themselves – so the process of story revision can continue like the images resulting in two mirrors being placed in front of each other – producing infinite 'reflections' of reality.

If you want to see the effect of this in action describe something from memory, a minute or two of activity to another person. Ask that person to pass on what they have been told to another. Almost immediately the story will be less elaborate; detail will be lost. As this information gets retold, say through the recollections of five or six people, the information will be almost totally corrupted; original detail will just get lost. But as detail declines people tend to make up for it by trying to make a story out of what information has been retained. So material is added to what is, by the time the memory is related to the sixth or seventh person, more of a story than a memory (although that is probably what a memory is from the get-go). At the same time stereotypes come into play as there are images we generate out of experience and information; hats, hairdos, glasses, rubber boots, dogs and walking sticks appear. The intentions of people referred to are added to, modified and subtracted – strangers to the tale appear apparently from nowhere; the story is added to, to make a new reality that suits and is explicable to the individuals concerned and the group as whole.

Now if we extrapolated from this kind of situation to, for example, someone witnessing a crime, we might expect exactly the same sort of pattern; immediately after the crime witnesses are starting to forget details of it. Every time it is related the event will be elaborated on. But after a period of weeks or perhaps months the witness is going to reach a point where the account has ossified to become the 'facts' of the event.

However, what is this 'product'? There are fragments of the event that are remembered quite accurately but bits have been forgotten. Unconsciously, or even consciously, parts of it have been inferred, things that 'must have been the case'. The memory is only partially true, which means overall, as a statement about what actually happened, it is false. This is what supervision is dealing with.

Flashbulb memories

Flashbulb memories are about where you were, what you were doing and who you were with when you first heard about a major public event. For example, the death of Princess Dianna and/or 9/11; the classic over the last half century has been the assassination of the American President John F Kennedy. A while ago there was a study of memories connecting to the Columbia space shuttle disaster. This tested the memory of people within a few days of Saturday 1 February 2003, the date of the tragedy, being shown on television. More tests were carried out two, three and four years later. The main finding was that there is a pretty swift decline in the information that can be recalled. However, after a few months this stabilises and what's left seems to stay in the memory for a long time. This means that our memories are a bit like plays written by us over a length of time, but once written they tend to become as factual as say the history of a President's murder; they become regarded by us as being our history and we tend to build our outlook on the future on the basis of this history, what we often call our experience. This being the case, reflection on or a review of experience is at once more than experience but also less than the actuality of the lived experience.

Conclusion

We, as human beings, are meaning-makers; we feel more secure with logic than mystery. Hence our experience becomes interpreted as parables or meaningful myths. It is probable that neither the supervisor nor the supervisee will ever know that what they are dealing with did not actually happen. Indeed, it is not unusual for supervisors and supervisees to report that they 'looked at what happened' or 'reflected on *the* situation'. Even more suspect, supervisors in training will relate to other supervisors the events and situations described to them by their supervisees. As you will now understand this is likely carry a shed load of inaccuracies and elaborations. You will also understand that much of what is being referred to in supervision will be completely wrong. Gaps left by forgotten material will filled by inferences. The more these are related, questioned by colleagues or reflected on, the more integrated in one's memory of the original account (which was inaccurate anyway) they become. In truth, what one is involved with is a seriously misleading situation. However, as Munro (2011a: 91–2, 6.30) seems to appreciate, we can be resistant to this truth, but we do need to allow for it in supervision:

Critical appraisal of the assessment and planning for a child and family, therefore, should be seen as central to good practice in reducing error. Ideally, this should be part of the culture and seen as not a personal attack but an outsider helping to pick up the unseen spots or offering a new angle on the problem. Supervision is one context in which this can happen: it should not be limited to this but something that colleagues or fellow professionals are able to do. The more punitive and defensive the culture, the harder it is for anyone to accept flaws in their reasoning.

The foundation of reflection and so the reflective practice that supervision is said to promote is memory, as reflection is essentially a process of looking back on our action; there is no way for humans to look back on aspects of our personal history without the use of memory. As this chapter has shown this basis of reflection is inherently erratic, subjective, judgemental, capricious and fickle. If you are still in any doubt that your memory is unreliable, ask a couple of people, who have been with one another from about half an hour to a couple of hours, to stand back to back. They can be friends or relatives, but it is important not to tell them what is going to happen before hand. When they are in position ask them to take turns in describing each other; the clothes they are wearing, eye colour, length of hair, jewellery, watch etc. It is not unusual for each person involved to be surprised how much the other gets wrong.

Memory is a bit like a snowfall. You look out your window in the morning and you see an unmarked sheet of whiteness – not a footmark on it. However, as soon as someone strolls over the snow it begins to discolour and go mushy. The more the snow is trodden on, the less it resembles the original undisturbed covering it once was. Memory is the same because it begins to alter as soon as others get involved; you can't really get the snow or the memory back to a pristine state. This needs to be a necessary elemental understanding within the supervision process if we are not to spend our time merely on storytelling. Supervision, if it is to be useful, must involve something much more than reflection. For Munro (2011: 109):

The role of supervision is crucial in supporting and embedding the new framework. Supervision offers reflective time and the practice framework encourages this through a critical and theoretical engagement with the child welfare issues.

The imperative elements here are the focus of a 'practice framework' that develops a 'critical and theoretical engagement' with what is primary and central to practice 'child welfare issues'. Here is an agenda which has the potential to cut down the leeway for distortion by way of memory and perceptions – it creates a corral of focus, which can facilitate a rational process of review, in that it provides a means to avoid or at least minimise meanderings into speculative memories. This 'framework' can be used as a means of keeping supervision as concrete as possible and on trajectory. For Munro (ibid.):

Good social work recording needs to be based on sound professional judgement and discretion around what is appropriate information to record based on the merits of the case, on a case by case basis.

This affords a method that can ground supervision; this is not impression but information based. It moves supervision away from being 'I think' led to being premised evidence (information). Perceptions and understanding can't be expunged from evidence, but they can be anchored to pertinent issues, processes, documented guidelines and shared expectations of practice. The use of directly recorded material (written or otherwise), photographs, videos can also be helpful. This might be thought of as a sort of more directed form of the cognitive interviewing approach (Fisher, 1992) a tool to gather information that uses quantity to achieve quality. This involves a close focus on parts of events, perhaps with the aid of relevant cues/prompts. The approach understands memory as a collection of many rooms and the cognitive interview functions as a means of opening the doors that the interviewee has previously unlocked. So 'I think' or 'it seems to me' are not flushed from the process, but they are not the conduit of supervision; supervision becomes understandable as a serious, quasi-legal process more than an ambling therapeutic, dislocated, largely undirected chat (or gossip). A further break to avoid this is provided by Munro (ibid.):

> Children and family have rights to know what is recorded, why and how recording is utilised in our judgements and ethical decision making.

This implies a need for a level of justification of what supervision is for, how it is mediated, what we say and share within the process. As such, supervision needs to be understood as a much more disciplined practice, set in critical review and engagement, something that might be partly facilitated by reflection but requires much more than merely reflective activity.

Our mind is like a city wherein new buildings, roads and subways are constantly being built. But like no other city, nothing is completely demolished or swept away. Spectres, ghosts and shadows of events and things can become solid as the light of concentration and consideration is cast on them. Humans essentially make their own histories and experiences out of the carnal world and facts are elusive within the process. Perhaps the best we can do is to be aware of this and try to make supervision less ephemeral than something that is run on memories of perceptions alone. However, if not, let us at least be conscious that what we are dealing with is more or less ethereal, something much more about whom we are than what we do. There seems little wrong with that because who we are tends to dictate what we do, but perhaps such work is better left to the realm of psychotherapy, storytelling workshops or amateur dramatics.

References

Bechtel, W. and Graham, G. (1999) *A Companion to Cognitive Science.* Wiley-Blackwell.

Brace, N.A, Pike, G.E., Kemp, R.I. and Turner, J. (2009) Eyewitness Identification Procedures and Stress: A Comparison of Live and Video Identification Procedures. *International Journal of Police Science and Management*, 11: 2, 183–92.

Bull, R., Valentine, T. and Williamson, T. (2009) *Handbook of Psychology of Investigative Interviewing: Current Developments and Future Directions.* Wiley-Blackwell.

Descartes, R. (2008) *Meditations on First Philosophy.* Cambridge University Press.

Fisher, R.P. (1992) *Memory-Enhancing Techniques for Investigative Interviewing: The Cognitive Interview.* Charles C Thomas.

Gigerenzer, G. (2002) *Reckoning with Risk: Learning to Live With Uncertainty*. Allen Lane.

Gilovich, T., Griffin D. and Kahneman, D. (Eds.) (2008) *Heuristics and Biases: The Psychology of Intuitive Judgment.* Cambridge University Press.

Goffman, E. (1959) *The Presentation of Self in Everyday Life*. Doubleday.

Masson, J.M. (1988) *Against Therapy: Emotional Tyranny and the Myth of Psychological Healing.* Atheneum.

Munro, E. (2011) *The Munro Review of Child Protection Interim Report: The Child's Journey.* DoE.

Munro, E. (2011a) *The Munro Review of Child Protection: Final Report. A child-centred System.* DoE.

Oakeshott, M. (1989) *The Voice of Liberal Learning.* Yale University Press.

Valentine, T., Brennen, T. and Bredart, S. (1995) *The Cognitive Psychology of Proper Names.* Routledge.

Waitley, D. (2004) *Empires of the Mind.* Nightingale Conaut.

Watson, E.R. (Ed.) (1924) *The Trial of Adolf Beck.* William Hodge.

Wilson, D. (2002) *Strangers to Ourselves: Discovering the Adaptive Unconscious*. Harvard University Press.

Wilson, T.D. and Schooler, J.N. (1991) *Thinking too Much: Introspection can Reduce Quality of Preferences and Decisions.* University of Virginia.

What is Supervision?

Brian Belton

Introduction

This chapter continues to develop a critical perspective on a particular strain of supervision. However, although I will be looking at a tradition of practice in youth work I believe the material has generic relevance, value and interest as an analytical critique of a practice which is generally agreed to, at least in part. This complies with what many writers see as a fundamental point of supervision – to apply critical analysis to practice.

Across the horizon of the practice the supervisor and supervisee might or might not be employed by the same organisation. Although there are a number of different supervision styles, the basic premise of the process, set in the sphere of professional activities, is framed within an agenda of concerns and issues relating to practice. Currently supervision is broadly understood to divide into two distinct arenas: managerial supervision, which is understood as largely concerned with performance and the pragmatics of every day practice and non-managerial (also known as non-formal) supervision that is broadly understood to be focused on feelings, reactions, attitude development and learning within an overall framework of reflective practice.

The arguments that are used in this chapter are based on a wide spectrum of reading (for example Tash, 1967; Kitto, 1986; Christian and Kitto, 1987; Reid and Westergaard, 2005; Shohet, 2007) my work with and training of hundreds of supervisors and supervisees, over close to 30 years and personal involvement over a similar period of time taking on both roles.

Model supervision

Compared to related disciplines (mentoring, counselling, psychotherapy, appraisal) and professions (medicine/health, social work, management) there really has not been a great deal of theoretical work undertaken about the nature and practice of non-managerial supervision (from now on what I will, for the most part of this chapter, refer to as 'supervision') in youth work. However, in youth work, the model of supervision has been reiterated, in slightly differing forms, for close to half a century. Over that period it has been replicated in the realm of academic training and the broad spectrum of services for youth all over Britain, but it is the fruits of this constant elaboration which constitute much of the material used in the training of supervisors and undergraduate students, what might be thought of as the orthodoxy of supervision. In some instances this has become to have a feel of dogma, as the stepping outside of its prescriptions sometimes provokes accusations of a kind of heresy. I am quite used to coming across 'supervision fundamentalists' who see it as a matter of principle that when a supervisee attends a session to 'open the door on time' (not a minute before, not a minute after) and never go beyond or fall-short of the 'supervision hour', no matter what other considerations might impose – departure from this credo, which in some circumstances is taken as the 'doctrine', can lead to 'book, bell and candle' – many have been 'excommunicated'. The offering of drinks, a choice of seating, opening and shutting curtains are other minefields in such company. While these are extreme examples of the 'priesthood' of supervision, rites and rituals, traditions and customs do apply, and arguments about such intricacies as note taking and sitting positions abound. There are supervisors who practice under strictures like, 'You *never* advise anyone what to do' or recite versions of the mantra 'I cannot impose my ideas on another person'. As such, supervisee questions about practice (or even the purpose of supervision) are frequently (and frustratingly) answered with a question; 'what do you think?' or 'why do you want to know?'

For all this, supervisor disapproval or disagreement can be effectively expressed, although in a disguised manner, by way of a puzzled expression and more questions; 'do you *really* think that?' 'what did you hope to achieve by that?' This is all done in the cause of supporting another often heard claim that supervisors make about themselves; 'I'm non-judgemental'. In terms of appropriate supervision, taking the stance of 'not-judging' is anything but helpful, as in nearly all cases, supervision is, by its context and purpose, about making judgements about supervisee practice and the supervisee developing their own professional judgement in order to become a more effective practitioner (able to deliver and maintain appropriate professional practice).

Much of this 'sacred modus operandi' is the creation of a web of myth or habit that is perpetuated by word of mouth as a sort of rumour of practice, as it is often not written down anywhere. Whilst the work of supervision has been repeatedly evaluated, that is, it is judged on its own terms (it proves itself to be a process of reflection) there has been no sustained, rigorous and critical analysis of this practice, premised on long-term comparative study of the outcomes of supervised practice, with the necessary control groups in place. At the same time the literature does not contain very much at all in the way of critiques of practice. This being the case the assertion that supervision 'works' or is 'effective' remains very much a hypothesis in the youth work field. However, it can't be understood as a working hypothesise as practitioners have avoided identifying possible flaws, apparently restricting the conduct of supervision to and effort to 'perfect' a given (custom and practice approved) model rather than examination of the same.

This is something of a loss, as the means of developing understanding of any subject or process is to develop a critique of it. However, prior to this book, this lack of critical perspective means that little evidence of the success or otherwise of supervision practice in the context of youth work has been generated. Most of the justification of supervision in youth work comes from collections of anecdotes, opinions and sometimes wild claims and groundless assertions (see Tash, 1967; Kitto, 1986; Christian and Kitto, 1987). As such, supervision lacks definite concrete examples of how, in some circumstances, it and it alone (as often seems to be argued) has 'improved practice'.

A common claim by supervisees about supervision is this it causes them 'to see things more clearly' or that they become 'more aware'. Another reoccurring rationale that individuals make for attending supervision is that it makes them 'feel better', in that it is a place where they can 'unload'. But this is all very subjective and what might be expected from adherents to any creed; the supervision 'church' (like any other 'ministry') has its 'faithful', ready to confirm its ethereal benefits. However, all that we can really say objectively is that as far as we know the delivery of service and provision to young people has not improved because of supervision. Indeed, as supervision has become more widespread in the youth service (since the late 1960s) it seems that the 'problems' associated with youth have deepened and become more prevalent. However, this is not to suggest that supervision has been the cause of the heightening of youth violence, substance abuse or teenage pregnancy up to the turn of the twenty-first century.

Although having a profile in a number of professional contexts, including medicine, counselling and social work, supervision has a common source. But the root is not (as has been suggested) in American voluntary work of the early part of the 20th century; the history of the tactical development of response based on the consideration of experience has a far older origin.

Observation, recording, prediction

Kitto (1986) writing about supervision, states that it has been around for more than two millennia, citing a warrior in antiquity questioning his presence at a battle. But the word/concept of 'supervision' is perhaps only noticeable by its absence in ancient texts. Nowhere is there a passage that says something like 'Ramesses II booked a supervision session with Nebuchadnezzar but could not make it because of a training event in the Nile Delta'. There are no details of this warrior signing a supervision contract that included attendance at a set number of sessions or making for a 'consistent' space or 'appropriate environment' to sit facing a supervisor for exactly an hour with his agenda at the ready. To say that this warrior was undertaking supervision is not too far from claiming that when a Native American family set up home on the shores of Lake George many hundreds of years before Columbus they were in fact taking out a mortgage.

In short, because Kitto (1986) says something does it mean that it is automatically true or even that it makes any kind of sense? Is there an investment in promoting supervision being always and forever present? There is nothing 'wrong' or 'bad' if the answer to both these questions is 'yes', but such possibilities need to be borne in mind when deciding if we are converted to/convinced by/believe in any given hypothesis. What is also necessary is some evidence for claims beyond what the likes of Kitto (1986) imagine, assume, fantasise, state or assert.

When looked at a bit more critically (rationally) we can often pretty quickly see that, for instance, while action based on reflection might be at least as old as civilisation, supervision is a relatively recent practice, often rather crudely (sometimes, almost delightfully, unconsciously) based on psychoanalytic principals that in practice pan out to be a somewhat covert form of quality assurance.

Foucault (1975) has argued that Bentham's 'panopticon' was the source of the adaptation of the scientific discipline to the social realm. For Foucault aspects of a range of techniques first formulated in the prison system have been adopted by modern professions. It was in that environment where the mass observation and recording of human behaviour (the activity of prisoners) was innovated as the scientific method enacted. One observes and records these observations that are the basis of predicting future behaviour. Why would we want to predict behaviour other than to create plans and preparations to meet it with 'appropriate' action in order that we will not be overcome by it? Foucault demonstrates that this strategy is an effort to manage possible consequences – management is the logical activity we undertake in order to control outcomes. In short, the process of observation, recording and prediction are undertaken to avoid, as much as possible, things getting out of hand; so behaviour might be *controlled.* This is a big contradiction in terms of the practice philosophy of supervision (the observing supervisor records their observations in order to make their supervision effective) that insists the process is about supervisees 'taking control' of their own practice. This is tied up in the maxim of the development of 'autonomy' in the supervision process.

The observation and recording function creates the form and means of reflective practice. As such, supervision has always been based on an 'us' – those that are doing the observation and recording on which reflection is premised, and a 'them' – those who are the focus of observation, recording and reflection. The 'them', the 'clients'/'supervisees' of today, were the 'enemy' or the 'criminal' of yesterday; those that need to be beaten, defeated, overcome, punished, reformed or controlled. This process has certainly been effective in the military realm and maybe, because a lack of alternatives, it has become part and parcel of all forms of detention in the industrialised world. But it is not obvious that what can be applied successfully in the 'them and us' sphere of war or prison can work equally well in the educational/welfare context.

This not suggesting that we see or think of those we work with in supervision as the 'foe' or 'prisoners'. Most of us have gone along with the ideas that are put forward to justify supervision – the 'person centred approach' a means of 'providing support', 'enabling', 'empowering' and 'developing practice' to name but a few. However, is that in fact what is happening? Is that what the supervision encounter is set up to do? For example, in the context of youth work, supervision (whether it is delivered as part of a college or training course, paid for by an agency or an individual practitioner) has a purpose that is set in what youth work does; the aims and objectives of the organisations and bodies that deliver practice, that reflect national and state aims and legislation. If this is not the case, if it is not connected to the day-to-day work, promoting whatever is taken at any given time as 'best practice', then the place of supervision is tangential; redundant in terms of its appropriateness or fraudulent (being an improper use of resources).

Making better and deficit

One of the most widespread models of supervision in youth work might be understood to have been established by Tash and later developed by the likes of Kitto. As such, the foundations of practice were set on backgrounds and/or training in group work and classic psychoanalysis/psychotherapy. This being the case, supervision is based on a general philosophy of interaction that is based on the notion of the 'talking cure' – a taken-for-granted presence of 'problems' and/or even pathology (neuroses). This has been transferred to supervision practice chiefly via the assumption that practice can be 'bettered' – it can literally 'get better'. This 'practice therapy' is realised by 'critical reflection' by the individual on their behaviour. Practice 'problems' or 'issues' are taken to supervision and explored. These 'issues' might be seen as mistakes or puzzles, but they are nearly always approached with an assumption, be this overt or underlying, that the situation presented might have been better managed by the supervisee; that their individual behaviour or response might have been 'better'. The hope that arises out of this exploration is that the next time a similar situation arises the supervisee will, because of their reflection in supervision, react more effectively or appropriately (better). The corollary of all this is the contention that 'learning' has taken place.

This is a subtle, but nevertheless inbuilt, deficit model; the supervisee, by definition, is 'lacking' (skill, knowledge, understanding, awareness) and they come to supervision to address this lack. The unsaid assumption on the other side is that the supervisor is not in the same condition; the supervisor has 'super-vision' and is type of 'guru' (see Christian and Kitto, 1987). This replicates the colonising aspects of youth work practice; agencies send out representatives into the 'community' to 'educate' or 'change' people who by definition are seen to need change or as relatively ignorant (being in need of education). It is not surprising that colonial influences continue to abide in youth work, as whether you perceive the practice to have its roots in welfare or education, British institutional culture was founded during the nation's long history of colonialism and association with slavery. This period, which is relatively recent (we continue to use the administrative systems and even the buildings of that time) and some would argue not yet over, given the persistence of economic colonialism and the UK's activity on the world stage.

Given this situation it is hardly surprising that there is much debate about the possibility of addressing the 'power differential' that exists between the supervisee and the supervisor, no matter how much the palliative that the supervisee is 'at the centre' is repeated. There is a clear differential in terms of influence and authority – one person is 'qualified' or 'certified' and often paid to 'assess practice', the other attends to be 'bettered' or to 'learn' and sometimes to become qualified.

In any of its incarnations, whether supervision is provided by way of agency funding, in-house networks, individual arrangement or in the academic setting, it is the supervisor's responsibility to listen to, examine and question (also called 'interrogate') what the supervisee brings to the process. The supervisor is thus making judgements, at least about what questions to ask, but when organisational funding, training outcomes or academic judgements are involved these judgements (the assessment) will be formalised in writing. Even when this is not the case, where supervision is paid for (in terms of time off or salary) it will need to be referred to and justified in terms of improved performance on the part of the supervisee and as such it is likely to be implicated in reports, quality assurance procedures and inspection processes. The supervisee, whilst assisting in the assessment is, in the main, the one who is being assessed; the onus is on the supervisee to 'produce' evidence (examples of their practice and how it is developing or how it may be improved).

Within this process the supervisor is not assessed on anything like the same level. The supervisor is often required to write a report about the supervisee while the latter is rarely asked to produce a report about the supervisor – assessment of the supervisor may be said to happen in a rather vague, informal, imprecise and ad hoc way – certainly feedback on supervisor performance is not common and in the main only happens if an assessment is derogatory.

The supervisor's assessment is in reality a report. This will be based on evidence that the supervisee has addressed certain criteria (that might be more or less overt). These criteria are specific to context, but in training and practice situations are related to what is widely accepted as 'good' or 'best practice'. Whatever type of supervision one is involved with, these criteria are always a factor as they will relate to what is understood to be ethical and proper in the field (however they are likely to be more obviously referred to in managerial/formal supervision). These notions of best practice are, in the main, responses to organisational funding requirements that are usually based on the dictates of government policy and legislation, although they might also be linked to moral and ethical predicates. This being the case, far from the supervisee being involved in framing their practice, the aims and targets of their work are well removed from their immediate influence – yes, they may have a choice of ways of meeting or achieving these aims and targets, but even this will need to fall within what is seen as 'appropriate' by legal/institutional/professional guidelines.

Autonomy

The room for 'autonomy' within the supervisory relationship (a consideration held dear in many youth work contexts) is, realistically, relatively limited. In fact the strictly autonomous practitioner, who did not adhere to the guidelines of best practice and did not fulfil required criteria imbedded in institutional and agency practice, would be regarded as something of a 'maverick' or 'loose cannon'. If this attitude was seen to persist, they would be undrestood to be professionally irresponsible; in the training context they would probably fail to be awarded a qualification – qualification being the result of proved knowledge of an approved cannon (an accepted paradigm or way of seeing the world of practice) and the evidenced conformity to a way of doing things that complies with this – one does not receive a qualification, promotion or any form of professional vindication by doing the opposite.

This is clearly the case despite what some individual workers might claim on the basis of what they see as their 'subversive', 'questioning' conduct or 'working within the system to change the system'; the nature of systems is that those who drive and thrive within them are those who most validate and perpetuate those systems – an enduring system tends to have the capacity to reject those who would undermine its survival while elevating those who propagate its effect and extend its authority. The longer an organisation lasts the more likely it is that it has recruited people that have helped it adapt to conditions. Hence individuals do not so much change organisations, but are changed by them, although an enduring organisation has a tendency to attract personnel who are equipped to fit into its particular evolutionary path. The classic motorcycle manufacturer BSA started out in 1863 as the gun manufacturer; 'Birmingham Small Arms'. The huge demand for motorcycles after the First World War (and the accompanying contraction in the arms market) meant BSA had to evolve or contract along with its market. It adapted to become the biggest manufacture of motorcycles in the world. In spite of the liquidation of Norton Villers Triumph in the late 1970s, the BSA brand history continues under the banner of Triumph Motorcycles up to the present day. BSA was able to build a future by fitting in with circumstances, not by recruiting people who acted in opposition to company policy. It achieved adaptation to circumstances by enlisting individuals who were able to enhance and add to the logic of that policy to enable paced redirection into diversification.

There are hundreds of examples of this kind of organisational adaptation and there are probably many more of organisations that have failed to find people who could help them adapt (which have of course perished). However, this history demonstrates that people tend to 'ride' systems rather than change them. Organisations might be understood as vehicles that either do or do not adapt to social, political and economic change. The individual who portrays themselves alone as the source of institutional change are, in the light of historical and social analysis, more likely to be labouring under ego inflation than anything else.

The very idea of having criteria to be fulfilled (as is the case in most organisations and agencies) suggests that there is need to conform rather than there being extensive space for the following of individual will or relatively unfettered personal autonomy. Successful organisational operation, in the main, relies on everyone in a given agency striving to meet expectations that involve addressing clear criteria to roughly the same extent (in the professional training setting this is embodied in the pass mark – to be given licence to practice; qualification).

Questions, statements, interrogation

It is commonly stated that supervision is not counselling. However, in the youth work context, the questioning that takes place, whereby the supervisor enquires and the supervisee responds, stays true to a counselling dynamic. The model, although maybe not always the practice, involves the supervisor asking lots of questions and the supervisee meeting this interrogation with their answers – making statements. I know this is quite a simplistic way of looking at it, but the naïve spectator to the 'supervision event' would be likely to see it this way. Usually the supervisor will make comparatively few statements. So one can see why supervision often claims some of the same sort of outcomes as counselling – higher awareness, problem-solving (supposedly without the influence of the supervisor – the answer 'comes from the supervisee').

As such, supervision is portrayed, at least informally, as an essentially caring or welfare role – wherein the supervisee is 'helped', 'assisted', becomes more 'enlightened' or is 'supported'. However, it is often claimed that none of this happens by the direct interjection of the supervisor, but somehow the supervisee achieves these ends via 'the process': this is all very mysterious and perhaps, to those uninitiated into the lore of supervision, preposterous. But is this what 'should' be happening? Is it in fact the case that these things are happening? Again, if an assessment of, or a report, written by the supervisor about the supervisee is the outcome (directly or indirectly) what is the purpose of this report? Well, it is focused on the supervisee's aptitude, ability, suitability, acceptability, appropriateness and the level to which they can be seen to have conformed to ideas of 'best practice', framed in the requirements and criteria of a given agency, institution or organisation, which, as noted above, are not conceived by the supervisee.

Quality assurance

The aims of the organisations that youth workers are employed by and their training institutions are mediated through national and international policy and legislation. To all intents and purposes this makes supervision a form of quality assurance, plain and simple. Now this is hardly ever overtly stated in any administrative or official sense. In youth work we seem to talk constantly of 'transparency', the need for 'honesty' and 'trust', both in terms of practice delivery of services and supervision. However, at the same time supervision and the function of the report/assessment of what has gone on in supervision, that is to make sure (as far as possible) that the supervisee is 'acceptable', is heavily camouflaged under the guise of 'support' (or whatever). That the resulting fiction appears to be believed by many supervisors does not make it any less deceptive.

The primary purpose of supervision is practitioner development. The exploration of learning and practice are not ends in themselves – this is in fact the material that is assessed; without this there is a lack of evidence of learning and practice. Without this body of evidence, assessment of practice would be limited to what could be 'taken in' by the osmosis of 'instinct' or 'feeling'. Indeed, I have read any number of supervisor assessments or reports that give little evidence of learning, expressing instead 'feelings' about supervisee 'growth' and 'development':

I felt Phyllis showed definite signs of feeling that she understands . . .

Georgie often gave the impression that he was becoming more aware on an informal level . . . he is on the same wavelength as young people and I have picked up that he is instinctively insightful.

Len has intimated that he has the mind-set to interpret formal learning into the informal realm.

All this gobbledegook might be part of the consequence of supervisors setting themselves up as having 'super-vision' or being 'gurus' but it is clearly a kind of erosion of commonsense into mystical nonsense and really does not help us in the quasi-legalistic work that qualification and practice is – where is the hard evidence in all this meandering claptrap to support or question whether someone should be trusted with the welfare and education of other people's children?

State purposes

Youth work is funded (directly and indirectly) and shaped (via legislation and qualification) by the state for state purposes, the same state that went to war in the Middle-East for the best part of the first decade of the 21st century without much in the way of consent from anybody. Modern forms of intervention into youth culture did not, as a number of writers have insisted, start with philanthropic/pedagogic/religious evangelistic activity of the 19th century; these interventions were of a wholly different order and purpose – they were piecemeal, in practice devoid of a national strategy or perspective, being largely uncoordinated forms of missionary work, politically-oriented activity or as expressions of humanistic morality. As such, with the possible exception of organisations like the Scouts, they were little more than localised bustle and hardly significant relative to state measures of the post-World War Two period, which were undertaken at a national level and framed within a loose but generic framework in terms of desired outcomes.

Community work was first mooted at a governmental level as possible means of addressing general social issues. This was predicated indirectly through Criminal Justice legislation of the 1960s. Youth work, as a mass, state funded and supported phenomenon, arose at about the same time, alongside mass immigration, the first post-war race riots and youth uprisings by the likes of the Mods and Rockers and later the so-called football hooligans. Before this time intervention into the lives of young people was relatively limited and certainly direct state interference outside school was relatively minimal. One of the main players in youth work in the last half century has been the Church, whose objectives derived from a spiritual rather than a political dimension. However the association between Church and State in the UK are pretty obvious, particularly given the head of the 'Anglican Sea' is also the head of state and it has direct representation in Parliament (the Archbishop of Canterbury, the Archbishop of York, the Bishops of London, Durham and Winchester and 21 other bishops in order of seniority together form the Lords Spiritual in the House of Lords).

From the 1960s state policy towards young people has fundamentally been about the channelling (or suppressing – depending on your standpoint) of youth activity and, particularly over the last decade, with the focus of practice set tightly on accreditation and skills, the production of a relatively flexible, comparatively compliant work force, so creating optimal conditions for capitalist enterprise. State funding (all but a relatively insignificant part of youth work is totally free from direct or indirect state funding) is provided for these purposes (try getting funding for 'having fun' in the current climate). The National Citizenship Scheme is the latest in a long line of initiatives directly initiated by the state (at a potentially tremendous cost to the exchequer – the 'Big Society' not withstanding) with 'national interests' as a motivation. This is what supervision acts to help contain and sustain.

I'm not saying this is what any of us in youth work spend the whole of our time doing – we work between the cracks – but the government is not funding youth work to produce rebels, questioning youth or potential revolutionaries as some youth workers and academics in the field might imagine.

Influenced supervision

The literature that refers specifically to supervision in the youth work sphere almost invariably does not, for the most part, appear to understand that the encounter is impacted by any and all the influences on practice. If they are considered at all, comment is limited to the odd, fairly vapid paragraph here and there. This writing, for the most part, portrays the supervisor/supervisee association in a sort of vacuum, focusing primarily or entirely on the disposition of the supervisee and their psychological reaction (via reflection) on practice incidents. Consideration of the environment is made incidental to this perspective; social conditions might be brought up, but they are often more or less portrayed as a backdrop to the supervisee's actions, feelings and their lay interpretations/assumptions about their clients, colleagues and their own psychological health/character (their 'paranoia', 'lack of self esteem'/confidence, their inappropriate 'attention seeking' etc.) which are interpreted as pivotal or more likely crucial to situations and events. The resulting 'sealed psychological chamber' creates a world wherein the supervisee is relatively detached from the nature of reality in a bubble of reflection. The realm is made up of memories, fantasies, reminiscences, nostalgia, grief, revelries, imaginings, assumptions, wonderings, wishes, hopes, fears, anxieties. They are sometimes, given the relative objective/accepting/'non-judgemental' (indulgent) stance of the supervisor, encouraged to take a seat on an attitudinal train with just three destinations; victimhood, persecution, saviour; many 'supervision stories' are versions of the same tale – 'he (I) did this to her (me) and she (I) saved/should have saved her'.

Fantasies and prejudices can arise from this mix (see Masson 1988). Following the encounter the supervisee emerges from supervisory mental 'tank' having manufactured a set of intentions, strategies, tactics and formulations in this detached realm to be enacted by way of their personal response to others, who are likely to know nothing of the accusations, postulations and totems built, given credibility and made 'real', during the supervision session. Unlike in the medical realm, which is clearly treatment-oriented, addressed to curing maladies, youth work supervision does not own this treatment function in the same way; that it is essentially focusing on something that is 'wrong' with people (supervisee or client) working out strategies designed to change individuals and groups (and even communities) for the 'better' without the imput and knowledge of the people targetted. This again exposes the underlying colonial influences on youth work.

This 'closed chamber' model of supervision (Figure 6.1) is unrealistic and as such unhelpful because supervision takes place in a context of which it is part; it is in no way of any significance detached from the same; it is embedded in its environment via funding arrangements, the need to meet aims and objectives and achieve prescribed outcomes that are often included in job descriptions and other employment related contracts as well as legislation and policy (local and national).

At the end of the day what college examination boards, employers and funders need to know from supervisors is whether they assess a supervisee to be competent to practice within their current or potential work context; practice, as defined by the profession, which is, albeit a multifaceted implement, a tool of the state.

In the last analysis the fact that those being supervised might feel supported or helped may be a good thing; it might motivate them to become supervisors themselves and take part in the dream; but perhaps if they were more aware of the bottom line of supervision they might not be persuaded to reveal as much about themselves as they do.

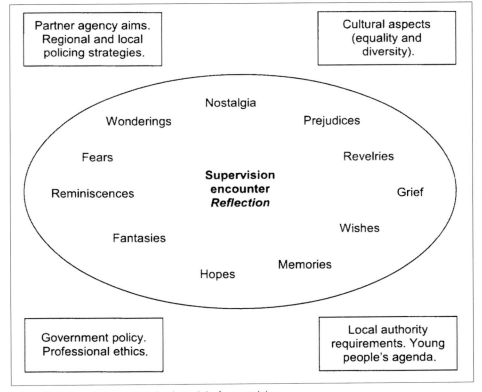

Figure 6.1   The 'closed chamber' model of supervision

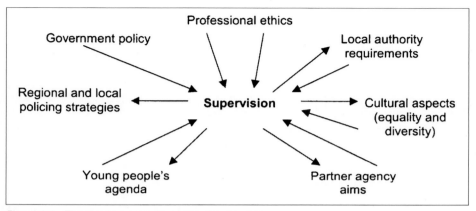

Figure 6.2 The 'world engaged' model of supervision

Checking and moulding 'best practice'

Supervision, which includes the processes by which supervisors produce evidenced about practice, is in fact quality assurance, because quality needs to be assured and measured (usually via 'transparent' criteria). This being the case, supervision does not produce 'better practice' of itself; it exists to check and mould 'best practice' and it is this that can produce improved youth work (meet the criteria associated with best practice or in the training context the learning outcomes that are associated with the achievement of what the field requires; employees who are able to address best practice norms).

That the supervisee goes away from the supervision encounter thinking they benefited from supervision might do little damage, but if that is all they see it as being about they have been deceived, which doesn't feel wholly harmless. They might walk away believing that what has been in effect an interrogation, that might in itself be educational, has just 'educated' them (they can 'identify learning'). They might not fully appreciate that they have also been 'checked out' and/or assessed on their compliance within particular frameworks and requirements, which they have little if any influence over, and as such are inherently undemocratic. Maybe this won't hurt, but perhaps it might not be altogether constructive. Beliefs that are based on illusions are dangerous in that they show how controllable we can be. If we do have a latent, internal power or personal authority maybe this can be made manifest in our ability to question these beliefs and so demonstrate our ability to take control/authority? We can at that point look to use our influence over supervision; make use of what supervision actually is rather than believing it to be something it isn't and can't be. If we, supervisors and supervisees, can achieve a clear and honest perspective of our role in the context of practice, then we might be able assert ourselves on the situation – this, I would suggest, is the dynamic moment wherein learning can take place.

Theory

As it stands, what passes for theory surrounding a widespread interpretation of supervision in youth work, owes much to the questionable values of what has become the traditional practice paradigm, which is made up of dated and relatively unexamined ideas. The extent to which any one of us might want to 'open up' to our supervisor (have our psychic world 'colonised' by an 'interested other') needs to be addressed, as does the question of how desirable, or even possible, it is for those we work with or just come into contact with for an hour or so every few weeks (a person we may not know particularly well) to have access to our most private and personal emotions/feelings/attitudes. On the other side of the supervision duality, how healthy is it for people, with little or no training in psychoanalytical or therapeutic techniques, to be operating this 'lay service'?

Managerial control

It is not unusual for those undergoing supervision to express an attitude that more of less equates to:

managerial supervision = bad, non-managerial supervision = good

This may have several motivations not least of which might be that supervision of the type modelled in Figure 6.2 provides something of a seductive form of escapism that is not present in forms of supervision that look more directly (overtly) at the quality of practice and outcome achievement. For all this, it is perhaps a reasonable organisational expectation that managers will be required to appraise and, in the context of the welfare/educational 'caring professions', seek to support those they manage. This of course constitutes rational and clear managerial control, which at its best will be set in sound logical procedures; a positive, authority-based role.

However, non-managerial supervisors are accountable to their 'funding client' and as such they also have a managerial authority or influence. This maybe more subtle and less obvious relative to the authority role of the 'named manager', but it is nevertheless incumbent on the non-managerial supervisor, if they are to continue to gain employment, to keep their basic focus on individual performance and the welfare of the organisation (the supervisee exists and to some extent is defined, as a supervisee, by their professional context).

This dynamic would of course be altered if the supervisor was paid directly by the supervisee (or if sessions were given for free) and the supervision encounter took place outside of work time, and was related to the supervisee outside of their professional context. But would this then be supervision? It might be more akin to counselling or even a form of therapy? Supervision to be supervision is surely set in and focused on practice (and practice will need to be related to organisational aims that arise from governmental policy). At foundation, supervision exists for workers to develop their practice; to find a way that they, personally, can operate whilst fitting into the traditions of the profession and the demands of employing organisations. The latter is invariably set within policy aims (due to the nature of funding) of the state. To this extent is supervision, at root, even in its most informal incarnation, much more than a quality assurance device?

This is not to say that many other 'things' might not go on within or grow from the supervision encounter; instruction, education, enlightenment, indoctrination, intrusion, nosiness, surveillance, enrichment, revelation, chat, gossip, epiphany, friendship, empathy, contempt, understanding, appreciation, repulsion and respect may all 'happen'. But supervision exists primarily as a process to review practice, and this is not purposeless at any level nor is it divorced from the social milieu by style or by the supervisor's relationship to a particular organisation.

Although the supervision process might, on superficial examination, seem to be based on the individual autonomy of the supervisee, the supervisor questions and encourages critical reflection about issues within a context set in a profession whose aims, training and funding are based on organisational objectives, which are derived from national policies, framed by state welfare/educational systems. This might be thought of as the paradigm of 'best practice'. But given its evolution and source, the trajectory of governmental policy is, at root, concerned with the production of a work force to facilitate the profit motive, which is central to maintenance of the market relations that are inherent in a capitalist society. That is the primary social function of youth work if not all youth workers.

As such, to understand the purpose and nature of supervision we need to go beyond the rather stale, contradictory and 'dog-eared' ideas such as many of those surrounding supervision practice adhere to and perpetuate. Through such activity our practice can develop and respond to current demands, without it there is a danger that it will stagnate and become increasingly irrelevant. For example, with regard to countering the rather worrying deficit model deployed widely in youth work practice (see Belton, 2009a, 2009b).

Developing paradigms

Although as Postman Pat said to Bob the Builder 'You can't fix everything', the relatively feeble grasp the youth work field has on the social and political forces that shape our work needs to be addressed; supervision, to be supervision, is surely set in and focused on practice (and practice will need to be related to organisational aims that arise from government policy). With this in mind the general picture provided of supervision practice is questionable as it remains relatively unexamined. There is a need to develop the current paradigm of supervision practice that often seems to deviate from its logical purposes. This feels, at least in part, because we seem to be largely in denial that supervision is part of practice that is driven by funding considerations, policy demands and organisational aims. As such, supervision wanders into the boggy swamps of half-informed naval gazing, camouflaged by vague references to therapeutic jargon and sometimes confused and contradictory claims made about the purpose and conse-quences of supervision.

An awareness of the need to draw on alternative theoretical dimensions to support a more solid direction to delivery is required, that can include a consciousness of the part played by organisations, funding priorities and wider policy implications in shaping practice. To continue to go along with the digression from supervision's inherent connection to policy implications and organisational purposes, into a quagmire of half informed counselling, bolstered by fuzzy referrals to a mystifying variety of therapeutic terminology, cannot better our practice or service delivery. The rather confused mixture of method and motivation for supervision that exists across the practice horizon does not feel helpful in terms of client experience. This is how Munro can be helpful.

How can the supervisor 'build-in' some kind of 'guarantee' of 'support'? What would be the consequence of such a commitment, especially given the diverse nature of possible support requirements and/or interpretation of the character/appropriateness and level of support? Is it not more realistic to consider the focus of supervision (the development of practice in terms of meeting organisational aims and care responsibilities) as the means of delivery of possible support (the channel/conduit/vehicle by which support might be delivered/accessed)? If this is the case it is also the contextual limit and potential of support available in the supervision encounter.

While supervision continues to be surrounded by a misty theoretical framework, shot through with questionable assumptions, some rather inane 'sound-bite' assertions and a few more of less unqualified generalisations, based on quasi-therapeutic ideas and, for the most part, almost antiquated perceptions of counselling structures, the means to move forward are stymied. It might be argued that this lack of exactitude and rigour invites collusive relationships rather than promotes collaborative encounters, premised on productive professional association.

An example of the lack of clarity in supervision terms is the claim that the start of the supervisory relationship is crucial, but what constitutes the 'start'? Is it perhaps the first session or might it be the first three? Surely the 'start' is relative to the length of time (number of sessions) that are scheduled to take place? Some people stay with the same supervisor for many years, as such the 'start' might equate to 10 or 12 meetings. At the same time, different people will see the 'start' in different ways; one person might see the first 20 minutes of the first session as the start, whilst another might feel that the first four sessions of a 12 session arrangement is the start. How would one know particularly before one 'starts'?

As the supervisory association continues, personal knowledge will be shared on both sides. This is seen by some writers to impinge on effective supervision. Does this mean that at some stage, presumably quite swiftly, perhaps before the 'end of the start', when a level of personal knowledge has been accrued on the part of either or both the supervisor and the supervisee, it would be prudent to end the supervision and seek out another situation wherein the level of personal knowledge is once more zero?

Another notion is that supervisees should not be uncomfortable. But should a focus of supervision be relative comfort? Should supervisees also feel 'cosy'? How can we know what is comfortable enough and what might fall into the realm of discomfort?

Some writers on supervision have suggested that it is best for supervisors not to have knowledge of the supervisee's work situation. But, it may be difficult to find appropriately qualified/experienced persons who live and work in a particular area who are completely ignorant of an organisation or its context and who know no one concerned with the same. However, are we, at least sometimes, more anxious about what we don't know than what we know? The mysterious might be seen as the basis of the many primal fears and imagination can be a far more industrious producer of anxiety than knowledge.

The discussion of the 'supervision contract' is another odd discourse that takes up a deal of time in the literature but a contract can have little real influence on matters. This is likely to be the case because what is called a 'supervision contract' is usually no more than a fairly informal agreement (that is all a contract is if not backed by legal force). This informality is confirmed as the supervision agreement usually cannot apply much in the way of sanctions if, at a particular point, it is not adhered to. It can also, with the consensus of both parties involved, be changed at a moment's notice (something not usually associated with the notion of contract).

More than establishing relatively meaningless contracts it might be as well for any supervisee to know why it is their supervisor wants to be a supervisor. It can be a form of voyeurism or a means for them learn about themselves by learning about others (you). They may just feel a lack in themselves so look to the lives of others (you) to fill the void. But they may just be involved for the fee.

Conclusion

In the last analysis, is not the 'bottom line' of supervision (as a general exercise) the development of practice to meet organisational aims more effectively, thus maximising the fulfilling of commitments to clients? Perhaps this is the limit and the potential apotheosis of any set of supervision encounters? That people in a supervisory association will know more or less about each other may well need managing, that they may have a contract that is an agreement or not, but the effort we expend on seeking to ensure mutual anonymity, or a perfect pact, even if these aims were possible, might need questioning, especially as this shared ignorance can never be more than momentary and a covenant is only as secure as its usefulness.

In practice many of us involved in supervision have realised the 'past sell-by date', paradoxical and well trodden nature of ideas surrounding practice and understand that it is by questioning this collapsing paradigm that our practice can develop and react to current demands. Without this kind of activity there is a danger that our role will fester and become increasingly immaterial. There are signs in the Munro Report, which promulgates supervision as a means of gaining knowledge, reviewing and critiquing practice and theory, as such proposing an active role for the supervisor, while placing evidence at the heart of a sensible educational routine, might bring a much needed sense of practical and disciplined direction. It is to be hoped that those of us in the field can make the most of the opportunity offered.

References

Bechtel, W. and Graham, G. (1999) *A Companion to Cognitive Science.* Wiley-Blackwell.

Belton, B. (2009a) *Radical Youth Work: Developing Critical Perspectives and Professional Judgement.* Russell House Publishing.

Belton, B. (2009b) *Developing Critical Youth Work Theory.* Sense Publishers.

Christian, C. and Kitto, J. (1987) *The Theory and Practice of Supervision.* YMCA George Williams College.

Foucault. M. (1975) *Discipline and Punishment; The Birth of the Prison.* Vintage Books.

Hawkins, P and Shohet, R. (2007) *Supervision in the Helping Professions.* Open University Press.

Kitto, J. (1986) Holding the Boundaries Centre of Professional Studies in Informal Education. In Reid, H.L. and Westergaard, J. (Eds.) *Providing Support and Supervision.* Routledge.

Reid, H. and Westergaard, J. (2005) *Providing Support and Supervision.* Routledge.

Shohet, R. (2007) *Passionate Supervision.* Jessica Kingsley.

Tash, M.J. (1967) *Supervision in Youth Work: The Report of a 2 Year Training Project in Which Selected Youth Workers Acquired Skills in Supervising.* London Council for Social Service.

Wilson, D. (2002) *Strangers to Ourselves: Discovering the Adaptive Unconscious.* Harvard University Press.

Wilson, T.D.and Schooler, J.W (1991) Thinking Too Much: Introspection Can Reduce the Quality of Preferences and Decisions. *Journal of Personality and Social Psychology*, 60: 2, 181–92.

Appendix 1: What is youth work?

Brian Belton

In the introduction to this book there is a general discussion about improving supervision, in any context, by learning from other professions; and a more specific discussion of how social workers might benefit from reading this book, which is mostly written by youth workers. The general view about learning from each other also underpins the inclusion of Chapter 2, which explores the relevance of supervision to the rapidly developing field of coaching, and in the process reinforces the case for a new paradigm of supervision in other areas.

The purpose of this appendix is to provide as clear a statement as possible about the character of youth work, the profession of many of this book's authors, to further help anyone in other professions to learn from the authors' experience.

It is not a root and branch explanation, which would risk precluding as much youth work as it might encompass, and I have not sought to demarcate barriers between what is and what is not youth work. What I have sought to do is draw out some of the distinctive elements that might distinguish any particular incarnation or profile of youth work practice, and include some brief indications of how this might develop and evolve. This is done to denote a basic direction for supervision in this field. If the reader of this book is a social worker or teacher they might note both common and distinctive ground, but, on the whole, they would recognise some of the elemental connections relevant to what might be thought of as a generic supervisory outlook.

The focus of youth work

Broadly speaking youth work develops within national contexts that have evolved in advanced or advancing welfare systems. It operates within and across the gaps between:

1. The everyday trials and pitfalls, joys and discovery of childhood and the responsibilities and duties of adulthood.
2. Forms of crucial personal and social intervention/care and custody and preventative activity in terms of safeguarding.
3. Personal development and risk of harm.

Points 2 and 3 above approximately mark out the boundaries traversed by youth work and social work.

Youth work can be generally defined as a profession practiced by those working with young people in a range of settings. Youth workers, worldwide, can be found working in clubs and detached (street based) settings, within social/welfare services, sports/ leisure provision, schools and, over the last decade or so, in museums, arts facilities, libraries, hospitals, leisure and sports centres, children's homes and young offenders' institutions.

The focus of youth work is on:

1. *The social education of young people*
   This is not usually simply forms of instruction, but includes a range of approaches, mostly developing learning opportunities out of everyday experience, including leisure and social pursuits, but also calling on more formal methods when appropriate.
2. *The well-being of young people*
   This includes attention to – and working with – young people, their parents, guardians and carers to understand, relate to and make use of their rights, and promoting and having concern for young people's welfare, while extending appropriate professional care.

The overall aim of youth work is to enhance the life experience of young people and their contribution to society as active, involved, useful and valued citizens.

Youth work in different cultural contexts

In Europe, youth workers can be found working directly for the government or local government, often involved in community development and community learning situations, building capacity, and providing forms of accredited and non-accredited learning. However, more and more, they are deployed by voluntary organisations (although via a range of funding arrangements, including direct and indirect state resources) in issue-related work (drugs, sexual health, homelessness, parenting etc.). Many such organisations, particularly faith-based groups, will be more focused on less directive and informal practice.

In Africa and Asia youth workers are likely to be working for non-governmental organisations in sport, arts, social welfare and health fields, and appreciable numbers will work in contexts similar to their European counterparts in the government/statutory sector, involved as youth service officers or youth volunteers within youth ministries, other ministries and departments.

Globally, youth work is a very diverse profession in terms of social tasks and employment situations. In recent years, with transnational economic and political changes, what youth workers do worldwide is becoming more similar. The demise of national youth services internationally, alongside cuts in state funding of welfare and capacity building services is likely to see a growth in the role of voluntary and faith organisations in youth work.

Youth work involves relating to, and taking a level of responsibility for, other people's children and the life direction of young people. Therefore it is fundamentally concerned and primarily focused on *care*. However, this care needs to be expressed in a suitably professional manner, which includes an appropriate level of detachment; youth workers are not 'big brothers or sisters' neither are they 'friends' (although they might be 'friendly') – nor is the youth work role a parenting one. So a professional detachment needs to be developed in terms of care

Given the cultural and national differences in legal requirements, age groupings and social expectations connected with the care of young people across countries and cultures, this care is often set within a framework of universal rights which can complement and underpin existing national legislation, practice, ethical and care standards/requirements. This means that youth workers not only need a working knowledge of childhood and human rights, but also the ability to interpret this knowledge and the associated principles into practice.

The profession of youth work

Youth work includes creating opportunities for young people to develop their individual and inter-relational capacities for personal and social benefit. This process serves to help young people become more self aware, but at the same time it provides part of the means for young people to make themselves understood by others to be a valuable resource in terms of the life of their society and the betterment of wider global society. This, being achieved within a framework of equality and democratic principles, requires the professional youth worker to be a 'social and political educator'.

Worldwide, youth work has traditionally been seen as a sort of secondary or 'para' profession in relation to occupations like teaching and social work; it has been understood as something of a luxury rather than a necessity. While youth work does have distinct skill sets and is informed by a range of theory and practice, claiming guiding principles and values, these do change over time, context and sometimes, even from person to person. Writers, academics and practitioners have reasoned this is because youth work is 'no one thing', but a combination of roles. However, others, looking to give the practice a greater level of integrity, purpose and perhaps status, have looked to provide youth work with a more definite grounding. This has, in some places, led to attempts to rename youth workers as 'youth support workers', 'youth development workers' or 'informal' or 'community' educators.

However, informal education is not a profession in its own right (there is no national or universally recognised professional body or set of parameters for informal education practice and you will see relatively few job advertisements asking specifically for an informal educator). In the main, informal education is a set of notional approaches, values and techniques applied in a number of settings, including schools and colleges, by a range of professionals. Its definition and emphasis seem to change over time, context and from person to person. Contemporaneously it has been embraced by youth workers, having picked up the label by way of professional training; and some writers have referred to 'professional informal educators', a title that means very little outside the academy walls as it does not really relate too readily to the role of the youth worker in law, the social expectations of the profession nor often the job descriptions. Taking a national and international perspective it is a fairly vague term and probably, with regard to being the raison d'etre of youth work, something of a fading paradigm as the split between informal and formal education becomes much more blurred than it was in the 1960s when the term was first used in any broad sense. Now youth workers use formal, non-formal, semi-formal and informal techniques and approaches interchangeably; indeed that might be thought of as part of the skill set of youth workers.

Overall, such titles have proved to be transitory and provide no clearer indication of the professional role. In fact they seem to give rise to ever more vague time, place and culture specific definitions of and justifications for practice.

Theories of youth work

There is very little critical literature relating to youth work. Most of what is written promotes and rationalises models of practice which are, in the main, based on heresy and stories, romantic and/or unconventional political views, guesses and assumptions. Such material often results in workers preaching homespun morality. This echoes the colonial/missionary era, which was underpinned by forms of instruction and domination. Over recent years there has been a growing awareness within youth work of the need to move away from this situation by avoiding simplistically telling new and trainee practitioners how to operate 'on' young people. It is becoming clear that if youth workers are to be of service to young people they are going to need to understand themselves more as servers (servants) than authority figures; youth workers exist professionally to work with young people to develop their influence and authority rather than merely to look to extend our authority over them.

At the same time, young people are portrayed as a group (as the colonial 'native' was) to be personally or socially lacking, deficient in terms of education, morality or even the civilising effects that can only be accessed with the aid of the 'informal educator' or 'youth development worker'. Youth, as a population group, are commonly depicted by way of assumptions, developed out of social fears, often inflamed by the media, about declining personal standards and moral degeneracy. The whole age group is frequently portrayed as in need of 'support', 'help', being beset by vaguely described psychological problems such as 'lacking self esteem' and 'attention deficit'. As such young people are contradictorily present, sometimes at the same time, as both a threatening 'enemy within', the seed of moral and social degeneracy, and as relatively incapable or infirmed group, in need of extensive adult and professional patronage.

This is a deficit model, which relies on convincing workers and young people that they (young people) have innate insufficiencies, that there is something inherently impaired in the condition of youth. This perspective is covertly oppressive, having its basis in what Franz Fanon, a psychiatrist, philosopher, activist and writer, working in the North African context, saw as the propagation of a 'colonial mentality'; that some population groups have 'inborn' inadequacies that need to be treated or compensated for by way of forms of social discipline or reformation (Fanon, 1965; 1967). South African anti-apartheid activist Steve Biko saw that convincing people that this lack was real was a means of the continuance of coercive domination. As he remarked 'The most potent weapon of the oppressor is the mind of the oppressed' (Biko, 1987). Echoing this is Bob Marley's plea, repeating Marcus Garvey's counsel to 'Emancipate yourselves from mental slavery recognising that none but ourselves can free our minds' (Marley, 1908).

Youth work, then, is based on a distinctly anti-colonial philosophy, but youth work is held back from developing as a profession because it is unable to clearly and succinctly articulate exactly what it aims to do and how it intends to do it. This does not mean youth work is intrinsically complex, but it does indicate that following contemporary western models of practice is problematical. There are many reasons for this. On the one hand, western states have looked to youth work to respond in pragmatic ways to demands driven by socio-economic necessity, developing a comparatively cheap, relatively flexible work force. On the other hand, historically and culturally, youth work has been shaped by moral, spiritual and political motivations, aimed at producing a more ethical and/or questioning population. This is what Indian scholar and author Shehzad Ahmed (2006) has described as 'Education versus Idealism' (Ahmed, 2006). In this situation the state looks to youth work to respond to regional, national or global conditions (largely economic) while at the same time youth workers focus on aims, primarily driven by personal values/feelings/points of view and often poorly informed political objectives. As such, youth workers have sometimes found themselves in conflict with management and state policy.

The key components of youth work

Care

Youth work, in common with social work, is subject to the expectation of a duty of care, so it involves the management of care. This is a concern for the welfare and well-being of others, but it is tempered by appropriate objectivity and thoughtfully sensitive detachment. This is not disinterest, but neither is it presumptuous. This is what youth workers need to do in their work.

It is probably a mistake for youth workers to think of themselves as professionals, as having 'relationships' with young people. The nature of the work is 'associative'; youth workers have a professional association with their clients (young people). Unlike lawyers or politicians, they do not 'represent' their clients; youth workers work *with* their clients in order that they might *represent themselves better* (as individuals and as a group):

- Youth workers are not nurses or doctors, so they are not looking to 'cure' or 'treat' people. Youth workers are not teachers, so they are not *centrally* concerned with forms of instruction, although the work might, from time to time encompass mentoring, leading or guiding; and youth workers will work with young people to become more knowledgeable and aware.
- Youth workers are not counsellors, therapists or social workers, but this does not preclude them from making referrals to such professionals if it is judged that this might be suitable or necessary. Not to do so might be understood as being unprofessional.

- Youth workers are not police officers, however we should be aware enough to know at what point we need to involve the police in our work.

An understanding of all this is encompassed in having the ability to extend appropriate care.

Social and political education

The approaches outlined above might be translated via an understanding of *social education*. This is the intellectual and personal means to interact and develop in the social context or according to Davies and Gibson (1967: 12) '... any individual's increased consciousness of themselves, their values, aptitudes and untapped resources and of the relevance of these to others. Social education enhances the individual's understanding of how to form mutually satisfying relationships'. This involves a search for the means to discover 'how to contribute to, as well as take from associations with others' (ibid.). It is a means to promote the interdependence of individuals, groups and communities for the benefit and well-being of all.

This approach shapes the activity of the youth worker, working with groups of people, creating situations that can enhance collective consciousness, working for social change collaboratively to advance positive development at local and national levels. As part of this, a sense of personal responsibility can be generated and the motivation for betterment of the self, but also an understanding of how this will contribute to the positive development of society.

Social education facilitates fundamental political education (democracy, representation, advocacy etc.).

Expectation

Youth work, framed within a professional context of social and political education and human rights, is anchored to a raft of expectations of both practitioner and client. The expectation of the youth worker is that they will have the ability to make professional judgments aligned to the aims, objectives and desired outcomes of their practice. However, we need to have expectations of young people in order that they might detect interest in and care about their well-being and that they might develop the motivation to have expectations of themselves.

In the west, much youth work has failed because of expectations being seen as a burden on young people; that they should be largely left to 'find their own feet' without 'pressure' (as if pressure might be expunged from life). This laissez-faire attitude has effectively abandoned many young people in terms of their wider socialisation; largely being left to their own devices, although supported by youth workers to take advantage of rights, entitlements and welfare benefits. However, because of the lack of expectations, many young people, having no real sense of duty (other than to themselves) and have been drawn into pockets of social selfishness, an 'all against all' attitude, which is ideal for the development of cultures of crime and disaffection (which is in some cases generations long).

Professional judgement

The nature of professional judgement starts with the understanding that youth workers, as practitioners, are not neutral; they are obliged to make judgements. A judgement is different to an assumption or an opinion; a judgement is an opinion based on evidence, the more evidence one has, the more secure one's judgement might be said to be. The more an opinion is made without evidence, the more likely it is that it will be prejudiced (a 'pre-judgement') or discriminatory.

It is important that youth workers are able to evidence professional judgement by demonstrating how and why they choose to do one thing rather than another. The worker, using a range of evidence drawn from their experience of practice, makes her professional judgement; it is a 'professional' judgement because it is based on practice experience rather than personal bias. Her judgement might have been good, not so good or even poor (depending, at least partly, on the outcome) but she had nevertheless used judgement because she had drawn on evidence; her action was not based wholly on supposition, feelings and what is sometimes vaguely called 'instinct', but on judgement built on evidence. This enabled her to make what might be considered to be an 'ethical choice' to take one course of action rather than another. This is something more than reflection, although reflection and consideration might be part of the process. Youth workers, as social and political educators, working within a rights framework, need not only to be able to make professional judgements, but work with young people in order that they might make effective judgements (ones that can be acted on) for the development and betterment of society.

Young people's participation

Central to the social educative response is the acknowledgement of the need for the professional *to be able to be taught about the wants and needs of young people by young people*. This is led by an understanding that the motivations, desires and passions of young people will likely be the richest seams of their future accomplishments and social contribution. In this approach, young people take the lead in learning within social education. It is the job of the youth worker to respond to this in an appropriate and adequate manner. This stance allows the young person to enable and empower themselves. Such an approach proceeds from the presumption that young people have, in the form of their integrity as human beings, potential, ability, influence, authority and power and as such is counter to colonial assumptions of deficit. Conversely, the professional who sets out to empower or enable others relies on inherently colonial attitudes, as this attitude assumes a lack of power and ability on the part of young people.

A practical definition for youth work

The aims of youth work practice need to be measurable and achievable. Vague and indeterminate terms need to be avoided. Looking at youth work worldwide, the following definition of its key purpose seems to express much of global practice:

Youth workers engage with young people that they (young people) might cultivate their innate abilities to develop their personal and human potential, in a holistic manner. Working alongside young people youth workers facilitate personal, social and educational advancement. This encompasses the political education of young people, developing their own voice and capacity to influence, and so take authority/responsibility, within society.

References

Ahmed, S. (2006) *Educational Thinkers in India.* Anmol Publications.

Biko, S. (1987) *I Write What I Like.* Heinemann International.

Davies, B. and Gibson, A. (1967) *The Social Education of the Adolescent.* University of London Press.

Fanon, F. (1965) *The Wretched of the Earth.* MacGibbon & Kee.

Fanon, F. (1967) *Black Skin White Mask.* Grove Press.

Garvey, M. (1938) *Black Man Magazine*, 3: 10, 7–11; quoted in Hill, R.A. and Bair, B. (Eds.) *The Marcus Garvey and Universal Negro Improvement Association Papers*, Vol. VII: November 1927–August 1940.

Marley, B. (1980) *Redemption Song.* MYV Networks.

Also available from Russell House Publishing
www.russellhouse.co.uk

Radical youth work
Developing critical perspectives and professional judgement

By Brian Belton

'**What a breath of fresh air to read this book.** It challenges the whole belief that someone can decide what is best for another person and then put in place what they think will bring the required change to make them into the "citizens they should be", and questions the way in which youth work has become a tool of government conformity, rather than a means of journeying alongside young people as they grow. *Not an easy or comfortable read as it pushes the brain to do some work, but definitely worth the effort.' Youthwork*

'The book is interesting and thought provoking, and should appeal to those social workers of a radical/critical persuasion, as well as those (many, I guess) who are unhappy with what social work became under the now departed Labour government.' *Professional Social Work*

'The lasting impression of the book is of someone who has genuine humanity in his approach to young people and a passion for youth work.' *Well-being*

978-1-905541-57-7